ASIS ASIS-CPP

Certified Protection Professional
Version: 1.0

QUESTION NO: 1

Which of the following is not a legitimate purpose of an investigation for employee misconduct?

A.
To determine whether company rules have been violated

B.
To ascertain whether company policies have been violated

C.
To catalog information about employees that might be derogatory for future use

D.
To determine if state laws have been violated

E.
To determine if federal laws have been violated

Answer: C
Explanation:

QUESTION NO: 2

The investigation's best approach to questioning relies on the following:

A.
Most suspects will lie or circumvent the truth.

B.
A suspect is innocent until proven guilty.

C.
A key suspect is guilty and evidence must be found.

D.
A signed statement in the form of a confession must be obtained.

E.
None of the above.

Answer: B
Explanation:

QUESTION NO: 3

Some facts about drug users that may assist in recognizing problem areas during a drug investigation are set forth as follows. Indicate the one that is erroneous.

A.
The only common characteristic is that drug abusers use drugs to a point where they feel they can no longer manage without its support.

B.
The adult abuser of drugs commonly has a history of social maladjustment.

C.
Drug abuse is concentrated in but not confined to "slum area of large cities.

D.
Those who can afford to buy drugs without resorting to crime are less likely to be arrested for drug violations.

E.
Chronic abuse of drugs is generally not considered a symptom of mental or emotional illness.

Answer: E
Explanation:

QUESTION NO: 4

A craving for a drug is exhibited often by the following:

A.
Water running from nose or eyes

B.
Frequent yawning or sneezing

C.
Continual itching of arms and legs

D.
All of the above

E.
None of the above

Answer: D
Explanation:

QUESTION NO: 5

A narcotic addict is sometimes called:

A.
A bingo

B.
A geezer

C.
A hophead

D.
A pop

E.
A bagman

Answer: C
Explanation:

QUESTION NO: 6

One whose sexual desires are directed to both men and women is known as a:

A.
Lesbian

B.
Bisexual

C.
Homosexual

D.
Transvestite

E.
None of the above

Answer: B
Explanation:

QUESTION NO: 7

When it is necessary to question a witness about sexual deviation all of the following should be avoided except:

A.
Using street language

B.
Giving the impression of being avid to develop the facts

C.
Leaving the impression you suspect subject of being a sex deviate

D.
Allowing the witness to frame the testimony in his or her own word

E.
None of the above

Answer: D
Explanation:

QUESTION NO: 8

In conducting gambling investigations, the security officer should:

A.
Cooperate with local, county, state, or federal law enforcement

B.
Not use undercover operatives

C.

Wiretap the employee's home phone

D.
Search the lockers of all suspects

E.
None of the above

Answer: A
Explanation:

QUESTION NO: 9

Which of the following investigative resources should not normally be used in a gambling investigation conducted by a proprietary investigative force?

A.
Closed-circuit TV cameras

B.
Undercover operatives

C.
Telephone surveillance

D.
Fluorescent powder

E.
Physical surveillances

Answer: C
Explanation:

QUESTION NO: 10

In an investigation concerning regulations of common carriers in interstate commerce or investigation of railroad accidents, a good source of information would be the:

A.

Federal Bureau of Investigation

B.
Bureau of Customs

C.
Federal Trade Commission

D.
Interstate Commerce Commission

E.
General Accounting Office

Answer: D
Explanation:

QUESTION NO: 11

In investigating homicide and suicide, the best source of information would probably be the:

A.
County coroner's office

B.
Health office

C.
State attorney general's office

D.
Federal Bureau of Investigation

E.
Sheriff's office

Answer: A
Explanation:

QUESTION NO: 12

To obtain information concerning marriage licenses, an investigator would contact the:

A.
Appropriate health department

B.
Tax bureau

C.
Bureau of Vital Statistics

D.
Appropriate court

E.
Social Security Office

Answer: C
Explanation:

QUESTION NO: 13

In conducting a "claim" investigation where the claim is a serious one and where there is cause for doubt in connection with the loss or claim, the type of investigation to be used is:

A.
Telephone

B.
Mail

C.
Personal contact

D.
Undercover

E.
Clandestine

Answer: C
Explanation:

QUESTION NO: 14

One of the following is not one of the desired characteristics of a statement obtained during a claim investigation:

A.
It should be written in ink or indelible pencil, or typed.

B.
It must be dated.

C.
It should be in short paragraphs with two spaces between each paragraph.

D.
It may be signed or unsigned.

E.
It must contain the identification of the person making it.

Answer: C
Explanation:

QUESTION NO: 15

A sudden, violent, and noisy eruption, outburst, or discharge by material acted upon with force, such as fire, shock, or electrical charge, which causes the material, either solid or liquid, to convert into gas and violently expand or burst is the definition of:

A.
A flash fire

B.
An explosion

C.
A detonation

D.
All of the above

E.
None of the above

Answer: D
Explanation:

QUESTION NO: 16

A yellow-colored crystalline solid pertains to the following explosive:

A.
TNT

B.
Dynamite

C.
Nitroglycerin

D.
Mercury fulminate

E.
Picric acid

Answer: E
Explanation:

QUESTION NO: 17

Which of the following is not a high explosive?

A.
Nitrocellulose

B.
Nitroglycerin

C.
Dynamite

D.
Nitro starch

E.

Picric acid

Answer: A
Explanation:

QUESTION NO: 18

Which of the following could be considered a source of information?

A.
A record

B.
A custodian of record

C.
A public official

D.
All of the above

E.
None of the above

Answer: D
Explanation:

QUESTION NO: 19

One of the following is not considered an element of the common law crime of arson:

A.
Commercial building

B.
Maliciousness

C.
Burning

D.

Willfulness

E.
Of another

Answer: A
Explanation:

QUESTION NO: 20

Which of the following is not usually applicable to a confession?

A.
It was voluntary.

B.
It was made subsequent to commission of a wrongful act.

C.
It is often applied to civil transactions.

D.
It gives no inference other than guilt.

E.
It is an admission of guilt.

Answer: C
Explanation:

QUESTION NO: 21

Which of the following is not a requirement for a successful undercover investigation?

A.
A qualified investigator

B.
A plausible cover story

C.

An effective control scheme

D.
Developing necessary evidence for prosecution

E.
A reliable method to discontinue or even suddenly abort the investigation

Answer: D
Explanation:

QUESTION NO: 22

If it is necessary to terminate an undercover investigation, one of the following actions should not be done:

A.
Withdraw agent safely

B.
Withdraw agent immediately

C.
Salvage as much of the resultant data as possible

D.
Prepare explanations for those who demand them

E.
Reveal the agent's identity

Answer: E
Explanation:

QUESTION NO: 23

The principal item of expense in an investigations budget will be:

A.

Communications

B.
Equipment

C.
Maintenance

D.
Personnel costs

E.
Training

Answer: A
Explanation:

QUESTION NO: 24

The single most important administrative control in handling investigations is:

A.
Indexing

B.
Case assignment

C.
Case review

D.
Documentation of status

E.
Case "ticklers"

Answer: A
Explanation:

QUESTION NO: 25

The frequency of a reinvestigation of the "financial lifestyle" inquiry should generally be:

A.
Never

B.
Every 6 months

C.
Every year

D.
Every 18 months

E.
Every 3 years

Answer: D
Explanation:

QUESTION NO: 26

In conducting interviews during an investigation concerning "financial lifestyle," the investigator should more appropriately tell the person being interviewed that the employee is:

A.
Being considered for a position B. Suspected of wrongdoing

B.
Being interviewed in connection with a position of trust

C.
Being considered for a promotion

D.
None of the above: tell the interviewee nothing

Answer: C
Explanation:

QUESTION NO: 27

One of the following is not prohibited by the Federal Civil Rights Act during an investigation:

A.
Asking questions about prior arrests

B.
Asking questions about prior convictions

C.
Directing inquiry into areas of race or color for discriminatory purposes

D.
Directing inquiry into areas of religion or sex for discriminatory purposes

E.
None of the above

Answer: B
Explanation:

QUESTION NO: 28

The age discrimination in the Employment Act of 1967 bans discrimination against workers or applicants who are:

A.
At least 35 but less than 60

B.
At least 45 but less than 70

C.
At least 50 but less than 70

D.
At least 30 but less than 60

E.
At least 40 but less than 65

Answer: E
Explanation:

QUESTION NO: 29

Questions on an application blank or field investigative inquiries that deal with a union membership or affiliation should be avoided as they may lead to charges that constitute violations of:

A.
The National Labor Relations Act

B.
The Civil Rights Act of 1964

C.
The Civil Rights Act of 1976

D.
The Fair Credit Reporting Act

E.
The Federal Tort Claims Act

Answer: A
Explanation:

QUESTION NO: 30

As a general rule the number of consecutive years of employment or nonemployment to be verified preceding the date of investigation is:

A.
5 years

B.
7 years

C.
3 years

D.
2 years

E.
10 years

Answer: B
Explanation:

QUESTION NO: 31

Any investigation containing unfavorable, information should be retained in a file for a period of not less than:

A.
1 year

B.
5 years

C.
3 years

D.
2 years

E.
10 years

Answer: C
Explanation:

QUESTION NO: 32

A question on an application form inquiring about prior arrests is illegal as a violation of:

A.
The National Labor Relations Act

B.
The Federal Tort Claim Act

C.
The Omnibus Crime Control Act

D.
The Federal Full Employment Act

Answer: D
Explanation:

QUESTION NO: 33

The rule that states that approximately one in ten applications will have major omissions, which will require going back to the applicant, is called:

A.
The Rule of Ten

B.
The Rule of Nine

C.
The 1-10 Rule

D.
The Verification Rule

E.
Sullivan's Rule

Answer: A
Explanation:

QUESTION NO: 34

Who of the following should be interviewed last or near the end of an investigation under usual circumstances?

A.
Those with extensive information

B.
Those preparing to take a trip out of the area

C.
Those likely to be hostile

D.
Those with less than extensive information

E.
Those only in the area temporarily

Answer: C
Explanation:

QUESTION NO: 35

If the interviewee during an investigation is hostile, it is preferable to conduct the interview at:

A.
The security office

B.
The home of the interviewee

C.
A neutral spot

D.
In an automobile

E.
At the office of the interviewee's lawyer

Answer: A
Explanation:

QUESTION NO: 36

Which of the following characterizations regarding investigative surveillance is not true?

A.
They are expensive.

B.
They are time-consuming.

C.
They are often nonproductive.

D.
They are illegal in most jurisdictions.

E.
They can be fixed or mobile.

Answer: D
Explanation:

QUESTION NO: 37

The process whereby communications are intercepted or recorded is known as:

A.
Physical surveillance

B.
Technical surveillance

C.
Surreptitious surveillance

D.
Black bag operations

E.
None of the above

Answer: B
Explanation:

QUESTION NO: 38

In situations in which at least one party to a communication is aware and willing that the recording of his or her conversation with another person or persons is being made, it is:

A.
A violation of the Omnibus Crime Control Act

B.
A violation of the Federal Communications Act

C.
Not a violation

D.
Allowed by the Federal Anti-Racketeering Statute

E.
Allowed by 18 USC 2511

Answer: C
Explanation:

QUESTION NO: 39

The specific emplacement of an agent or operative in an environment or situation in which the agent's true role is unknown with the purpose of developing information to be used later in a criminal investigation is known as:

A.
Closed investigation

B.
Secret investigation

C.
Technical investigation

D.
Concealed investigation

E.
Undercover investigation

Answer: E
Explanation:

QUESTION NO: 40

It is becoming increasingly more difficult to do a good preemployment background investigation because of:

A.
The expense

B.
The lack of skilled investigators

C.
Various rulings and court decisions that inhibit the use of techniques or instruments available

D.
The uncooperative attitudes of persons interviewed

E.
Such investigations are illegal in a number of states

Answer: C
Explanation:

QUESTION NO: 41

Which of the following is an advantage of having investigation conducted by in-house security staff?

A.
Cheaper as a general rule, depending on number of check being done

B.
In-house staff is better trained

C.
In-house staff has better grasp as to objective of the investigation

D.
In-house staff has better sources of information

E.
None of the above

Answer: C
Explanation:

QUESTION NO: 42

The most widely recognized and best-known instrument designed to detect deception is:

A.
Fingerprint classifier

B.
Voice analyzer

C.
Polygraph

D.
Truth serum

E.
Stress analyzer

Answer: C
Explanation:

QUESTION NO: 43

The most important factor in the use of a polygraph is:

A.
The examiner

B.
The make of the instrument

C.
Environmental factors

D.
The time of day

E.
The types of questions

Answer: A

Explanation:

QUESTION NO: 44

Which of the following is not a good procedure with regard to the use of the polygraph by investigators?

A.
Pointing out its effectiveness

B.
Describing it as infallible

C.
Withholding detailed information from the examinee

D.
Telling the examinee how experienced the examiner is

E.
Working with the examiner as a team member

Answer: B
Explanation:

QUESTION NO: 45

The U.S. Army trains its polygraph operators as well as those from other U.S. agencies at:

A.
West Point, New York

B.
Washington, D.C.

C.
Fort Gordon, Georgia

D.
Fort Leavenworth, Kansas

E.
Fort Meade, Maryland

Answer: C
Explanation:

QUESTION NO: 46

A device used to detect deception through stress recorded by voice modulations is known as (a):

A.
Polygraph

B.
Lie detector

C.
Psychological stress analyzer

D.
Truth serum

E.
Hypnotism

Answer: C
Explanation:

QUESTION NO: 47

Which of the following characteristics relate to the psychological stress analyzer?

A.
No physical connection with the body is required.

B.
The subject is not required to answer in a terse "yes" or "no" format.

C.
It can be used covertly.

D.
All of the above.

E.
None of the above.

Answer: D
Explanation:

QUESTION NO: 48

The effectiveness of the voice analyzer in accurately detecting deception is:

A.
100 percent

B.
96 percent

C.
94 percent

D.
85 percent

E.
Not determined

Answer: E
Explanation:

QUESTION NO: 49

Identify the Act that basically prohibits discrimination, discharge, failure or refusal to hire, etc., on any of the grounds of race, color, religion, sex, or national origin:

A.
The Fair Credit Reporting Act

B.

The Civil Rights Act of 1964

C.
The First Amendment

D.
The Omnibus Crime Control Act

E.
None of the above

Answer: B
Explanation:

QUESTION NO: 50

Under court interpretations of the Civil Rights Act of 1964, which of the following are not allowed during investigations?

A.
Questions regarding prior arrests

B.
Questions regarding prior convictions

C.
Questions regarding age

D.
Questions regarding residence

E.
Questions regarding prior employment

Answer: A
Explanation:

QUESTION NO: 51

Interviews should be conducted:

A.
In the company of the suspect's attorney

B.
In an area where distractions are minimal

C.
In a comfortable room that is well furnished like home

D.
In an area where the light is focused on the suspect's face

E.
None of the above

Answer: B
Explanation:

QUESTION NO: 52

The witness's idea of the suspect, described in words, is called:

A.
Portrait parle

B.
Modus operandi

C.
Corpus delecti

D.
All of the above

E.
None of the above

Answer: A
Explanation:

QUESTION NO: 53

The most important qualification of a good undercover operator is:

A.
Resourcefulness

B.
Education

C.
Experience

D.
Good contacts

E.
None of the above

Answer: A
Explanation:

QUESTION NO: 54

The main function of the private security agent is to:

A.
Locate stolen goods

B.
Ascertain and report illegal activities

C.
Receive well-rounded investigative experience

D.
Ascertain the state of morale

E.
None of the above

Answer: B
Explanation:

QUESTION NO: 55

The person best suited for physical surveillance work is one who:

A.
Is tall enough to see over crowds

B.
Will blend into the area

C.
Has a college education

D.
Has a background of police work

E.
None of the above

Answer: B
Explanation:

QUESTION NO: 56

In conducting a polygraph, it is important to note that the most important measure of stress is recorded by:

A.
Breathing

B.
Galvanic skin response

C.
Heartbeats

D.
Perspiration

E.
None of the above

Answer: C

Explanation:

QUESTION NO: 57

The pre-testing interview prior to the polygraph examination itself is for the purpose of:

A.
Helping the subject to relax

B.
Helping the examiner to get to know the subject

C.
Helping the examiner to judge the subject's character

D.
All of the above

E.
None of the above

Answer: D
Explanation:

QUESTION NO: 58

On average, a polygraph examination takes:

A.
10 hours

B.
1 hour

C.
15 minutes

D.
5 hours I

E.
4 hours

Answer: B
Explanation:

QUESTION NO: 59

Which of the following statements is not correct regarding the polygraph?

A.
The polygraph is not a lie detector.

B.
The polygraph does not automatically register truth or falsehood.

C.
A polygraph test is conclusive.

D.
Historically, polygraphs have more often been used to establish innocence rather than to prove guilt.

E.
None of the above.

Answer: C
Explanation:

QUESTION NO: 60

Persons are protected from abuses of polygraph by:

A.
The courts through civil lawsuits

B.
State labor departments

C.
The National Labor Relations Board

D.
All of the above

E.
None of the above

Answer: D
Explanation:

QUESTION NO: 61

The best way to verify an applicant's statements is:

A.
By judicious use of the telephone

B.
By a personal visit with the applicant

C.
By mail

D.
All of the above

E.
None of the above

Answer: E
Explanation:

QUESTION NO: 62

Which of the following should not be included in the written investigative report of an applicant?

A.
Derogatory information

B.
Confidential sources of information

C.
Results of a lie detector examination

D.
Arrest records

E.
None of the above

Answer: B
Explanation:

QUESTION NO: 63

Of all those with mental disorders, the most dangerous subject to handle is:

A.
One suffering hysteria

B.
A paranoid psychotic

C.
A neurotic

D.
One suffering phobia

E.
Schizophrenic

Answer: B
Explanation:

QUESTION NO: 64

Mental disorders may be determined by symptoms. Which of the following is such a symptom?

A.
Sudden changes in behavior

B.
Behavior that is not harmonious with a situation

C.
Unduly prolonged depression

D.
All of the above

E.
None of the above

Answer: D
Explanation:

QUESTION NO: 65

In handling a mentally disturbed person, one should:

A.
Take a strong position as the boss

B.
Assume a calm and friendly position

C.
Leave the impression he or she has control of the situation

D.
All of the above

E.
None of the above

Answer: B
Explanation:

QUESTION NO: 66

Which of the following is true in handling persons with mental disorders?

A.
Don't deceive them.

B.
Don't become involved in their personal problems.

C.
Where physical restraint is required, use two officers.

D.
All of the above.

E.
None of the above.

Answer: D
Explanation:

QUESTION NO: 67

The purpose for employing an access control program includes:

A.
To protect persons, materials, or information

B.
To slow or speed up the rate of movement to, from, or within an establishment

C.
To permit or deny entrance

D.
Both A and C

E.
All of the above

Answer: E
Explanation:

QUESTION NO: 68

Identification and access control systems have the widest application of:

A.
Manual identification systems

B.
Magnetic readers

C.
Biometric-based systems

D.
Dielectric readers

E.
None of the above

Answer: A
Explanation:

QUESTION NO: 69

The performance requirements of any trustworthy system of identification includes:

A.
Resistance to surreptitious substitution or counterfeiting

B.
Reliability

C.
Validity

D.
Both B and C

E.
All of the above

Answer: E
Explanation:

QUESTION NO: 70

A general defect of manual identification systems is that:

A.
Many are made of plastic.

B.
Many do not have biometric characteristics on them.

C.
Once issued, they tend to remain valid indefinitely.

D.
They lack identifying colors.

E.
None of the above.

Answer: C
Explanation:

QUESTION NO: 71

Any formula, pattern, device, or compilation of information that is used in one's business and that gives you an opportunity to gain an advantage over competitors who do not use it or know about it is:

A.
A patent

B.
A trade secret

C.
A monopoly

D.
Copyrighted material

E.
None of the above

Answer: B
Explanation:

QUESTION NO: 72

What is most likely the main reason for loss of sensitive information?

A.
Industrial espionage

B.
An employee's loose lips

C.
Inadvertent disclosure

D.
Deliberate theft by an outsider

E.
Both B and C

F.
None of the above

Answer: E
Explanation:

QUESTION NO: 73

Which of the following should be part of an effective information security program?

A.
Pre-employment screening

B.
Nondisclosure agreements from employees

C.
Employee awareness programs

D.
Policy and procedural statements on the recognition, classification, and handling of sensitive information

E.

All of the above

Answer: E
Explanation:

QUESTION NO: 74

The primary tool of pre-employment screening is the:

A.
Application form

B.
Interview

C.
Polygraph

D.
Investigator performing the interview

Answer: A
Explanation:

QUESTION NO: 75

Which of the following is generally not allowed to be disclosed on an employment questionnaire?

A.
Current residence

B.
References

C.
Prior employment

D.
Prior arrests

E.

None of the above

Answer: D
Explanation:

QUESTION NO: 76

To be within the definition of a trade secret, sensitive information must meet which of the following criteria?

A.
Individuals to whom it is disclosed must know it is secret.

B.
It must be identifiable.

C.
It must not be already available in public sources.

D.
There must be some obvious indication that the owner is attempting to prevent its unauthorized disclosure.

E.
a, c, and d.

F.
All of the above.

Answer: E
Explanation:

QUESTION NO: 77

According to the "restatement of the law of torts," a trade secret is:

A.
All information about a company that the company desires to protect

B.
Any formula, pattern, device, or compilation of information that is used in one's business and that

gives that business an opportunity to gain an advantage over competitors who do not know or use it

C.
Information about a company that is registered with the U.S. Patent Office

D.
Both A and B

E.
All of the above

Answer: B
Explanation:

QUESTION NO: 78

A trade secret may be:

A.
A formula for a chemical compound

B.
A process of manufacturing materials

C.
A pattern for a machine

D.
A list of customers

E.
All of the above

Answer: E
Explanation:

QUESTION NO: 79

The characteristics of a trade secret as compared with other confidential information are:

A.
Those business secrets that have been duly registered pursuant to the requirements of law

B.
Continuous or consistent business applications of a secret not known to others, from the use of which some advantage is gained by the user

C.
Those business secrets that are fully protected in accordance with the Federal Privacy Act

D.
Both A and C

E.
All of the above

Answer: B
Explanation:

QUESTION NO: 80

Which of the following is generally not true in regard to trade secrets?

A.
The more a business narrowly defines what it regards as a secret, the easier it is to protect that body of information.

B.
It is difficult to protect a trade secret that can be found in publicly accessible sources.

C.
Secret information does have to be specifically identifiable.

D.
Secret information must be effectively protected.

E.
None of the above.

Answer: E
Explanation:

QUESTION NO: 81

In regard to a trade secret, it may be decided that its disclosure by another was innocent, rather than wrongful, even in the case where the person making the disclosure really was guilty of malice or wrong intent. This situation may occur when:

A.
The trade secret was not registered

B.
The trade secret did not involve national defense information

C.
The trade secret was not in current use

D.
There is absence of evidence that an owner has taken reason- able precautions to protect confidential information.

E.
All of the above

Answer: D
Explanation:

QUESTION NO: 82

Proprietary information is:

A.
Private information of a highly sensitive nature

B.
Information that must be classified according to executive order of the U.S. Government

C.
Sensitive information that is classified according to executive order of the U.S. Government

D.
Anything that an enterprise considers relevant to its status or opera

Answer: D
Explanation:

QUESTION NO: 83

The class of person under a duty to safeguard a proprietary secret is known as a(n):

A.
Agent

B.
Proprietary security employee

C.
Fiduciary

D.
Business associate

E.
None of the above

Answer: C
Explanation:

QUESTION NO: 84

It is important for employees to know whether confidential information is a trade secret, or some other confidential material, because:

A.
If it is a trade secret, the employee may be prevented from disclosing t by injunction.

B.
If not a trade secret and it is disclosed, the employer must take action after the disclosure and must be able to prove some actual damage in order to recover

C.
If not a trade secret, the information once disclosed is no longer defendable

D.
If not a trade secret, the information once disclosed cannot be further prevented from disclosure by an injunction

E.
All of the above.

Answer: E
Explanation:

QUESTION NO: 85

Which of the following is not a correct statement as a general rule involving the protection of proprietary information?

A.
As a class, employees are the largest group of persons bound to secrecy because of their status or relationship

B.
By operation of common law, employees are presumed to be fiduciaries to an extent that they may not disclose secrets of their employers without authorization

C.
Other than the employees, any other persons to be bound to secrecy must agree to be so bound

D.
Any agreements to be bound must always be in writing and are not implied from acts

Answer: D
Explanation:

QUESTION NO: 86

To effectively involve the law for the protection of sensitive information, the owner of the proprietary information must be able to show "objective indications of attempts to protect secrecy." Which of the following has been recognized in the past as such an indication?

A.
Use of warning signs to alert employees to sensitive data and the places it is stored

B.
Separately storing sensitive information in security containers with the appropriate security precautions

C.
Special instructions providing a "need-to-know" basis

D.

Restrictions to nonemployee access to places containing sensitive information

E.
All of the above

Answer: E
Explanation:

QUESTION NO: 87

Which of the following should be made part of a proprietary information protection program?

A.
Pre-employment screening

B.
Effective perimeter control system

C.
Execution of patent and secrecy agreement

D.
Paper and data control

E.
Both A and C

F.
All of the above

Answer: F
Explanation:

QUESTION NO: 88

In designing a proprietary information protection program, the area of greatest vulnerability is:

A.
Personnel files

B.

Employees

C.
Computers

D.
Marketing data

E.
Perimeter boundaries

Answer: B
Explanation:

QUESTION NO: 89

In devising proprietary information procedures, which of the following is considered to be a main area of paper or document vulnerability?

A.
Comprehensive paper controls

B.
A technical report system

C.
Control and issue of notebooks

D.
All of the above

E.
None of the above

Answer: B
Explanation:

QUESTION NO: 90

When a loss of proprietary information is discovered, which of the following steps should be taken first?

A.
Attempt to recover the material.

B.
Attempt to apprehend the perpetrators.

C.
Assess economic damage.

D.
Re-evaluate the protection system.

E.
All of the above.

Answer: E
Explanation:

QUESTION NO: 91

Which of the following would not be considered in the "trade secret" category?

A.
Salary data

B.
Market surveys

C.
Personnel matters

D.
Customer usage evaluations

E.
All of the above

Answer: E
Explanation:

QUESTION NO: 92

Litigations concerning former employees involving trade secrets have some problems. Which of the following is considered to be such a problem?

A.
The cost of litigations is too high and the owner of the trade secret may lose.

B.
Litigation is a waste of time.

C.
The owner of the trade secret may have to expose the information that is being protected.

D.
Both A and C.

E.
All of the above.

Answer: D
Explanation:

QUESTION NO: 93

A "trash cover" is:

A.
A sealed cover on a trash container

B.
The process of examining one's trash for information

C.
Placing the company's trash in a locked container

D.
Both A and C

E.
All of the above

Answer: B
Explanation:

QUESTION NO: 94

Sound waves too high in frequency to be heard by the human ear, generally above 20 kHz, are known as:

A.
High-frequency sound waves

B.
Microwave waves

C.
Ultrasonic waves

D.
Short-frequency sound waves

E.
None of the above

Answer: C
Explanation:

QUESTION NO: 95

The process of combining a number of transmission into one composite signal to be sent over one link is called:

A.
Transmission integrity

B.
Communication integration

C.
A demultiplexer

D.
Multiplexing

E.
None of the above

Answer: D

Explanation:

QUESTION NO: 96

Which of the following applies to the laser as a means of communication?

A.
Line of sight transmission is necessary.

B.
Poor weather conditions interfere with the beam.

C.
It is practically impossible to intercept the beam without detection.

D.
Both A and C.

E.
All of the above.

Answer: E
Explanation:

QUESTION NO: 97

Which of the following is not correct in regard to microwave transmissions?

A.
Microwave signals penetrate fog and snow.

B.
Microwave signals are transmitted in short radio waves.

C.
A large number of microwave signals can be transmitted.

D.
Microwave signals travel in curved lines.

E.
Microwave signals are not affected by ordinary man-made noise.

F.
None of the above.

Answer: D
Explanation:

QUESTION NO: 98

Electromagnetic radiation is detectable electromagnetic energy that is generated by electronic information processing devices. Which' of the following is used to protect very sensitive equipment?

A.
A current carrier device

B.
Pneumatic cavity shielding

C.
Tempest shielding

D.
Pen register shielding

Answer: C
Explanation:

QUESTION NO: 99

The practice of preventing unauthorized persons from gaining information by analyzing electromagnetic emanations from electronic equipment is often termed:

A.
Bugging

B.
Veiling

C.

Tempest

D.
All of the above

E.
None of the above

Answer: C
Explanation:

QUESTION NO: 100

A term used to indicate a method of disguising information so that it is unintelligible to those who should not obtain it is:

A.
Interconnection decoy

B.
Multiplexing

C.
Scrambling

D.
Mixed signal

E.
None of the above

Answer: C
Explanation:

QUESTION NO: 101

The most secure scrambler in common use is the:

A.
Frequency inverter

B.
Decoder

C.
Laser beam

D.
Vocoder

E.
None of the above

Answer: D
Explanation:

QUESTION NO: 102

The method used to monitor telephone calls by providing a record of all numbers dialed from a particular phone is called:

A.
Electronic surveillance

B.
Phone bug

C.
Wiretap

D.
Pen register

E.
None of the above

Answer: D
Explanation:

QUESTION NO: 103

A small hidden microphone and a radio transmitter are generally known as:

A.
A wiretap

B.
A bug

C.
A beeper

D.
Electronic surveillance

E.
All of the above

Answer: B
Explanation:

QUESTION NO: 104

A specially constructed microphone attached directly to an object or surface to be protected, which responds only when the protected object or surface is disturbed, is known as:

A.
Parabolic microphone

B.
Special audio microphone

C.
Contact microphone

D.
Surreptitious microphone

E.
None of the above

Answer: C
Explanation:

QUESTION NO: 105

ASIS ASIS-CPP Exam

A microphone with a disklike attachment that is used for listening to audio from great distances is known as a(n):

A.
Contact microphone

B.
Parabolic microphone

C.
Ultrasonic microphone

D.
Both A and C

E.
None of the above

Answer: B
Explanation:

QUESTION NO: 106

A microphone that is installed on a common wall adjacent to the target area when it is impractical or impossible to enter the target area is known as a:

A.
Carbon microphone

B.
Parabolic microphone

C.
Contact microphone

D.
Dynamic microphone

E.
None of the above

Answer: C
Explanation:

QUESTION NO: 107

Which method of protection against telephone line eavesdropping is most reliable?

A.
Don't discuss sensitive information.

B.
Use a radio jammer.

C.
Use encryption equipment.

D.
Both A and C.

E.
Use an audio jammer.

Answer: D
Explanation:

QUESTION NO: 108

The unauthorized acquisition or dissemination by an employee of confidential data critical to his or her employer is known as:

A.
Embezzlement

B.
Larceny

C.
Industrial espionage

D.
Burglary

E.
False pretenses

Answer: C
Explanation:

QUESTION NO: 109

The term "eavesdropping" refers to:

A.
Wiretapping

B.
Bugging

C.
Trash cover

D.
Both A and C

E.
All of the above

Answer: D
Explanation:

QUESTION NO: 110

Which of the following methods could be used as a form of eavesdropping using a telephone instrument?

A.
Wiring can be altered so the handset or receiver will act as an open microphone.

B.
A radio transmitter can be concealed in the mouthpiece.

C.
The infinity transmitter can be used.

D.
Both B and C.

E.
All of the above.

Answer: E
Explanation:

QUESTION NO: 111

A microphone that requires no power source, is very small, and is difficult to detect has the characteristics of a(n):

A.
Contact microphone

B.
Parabolic microphone

C.
Dynamic microphone

D.
Infinity microphone

E.
None of the above

Answer: C
Explanation:

QUESTION NO: 112

Installation of a wireless radio eavesdropping device usually consists of the following:

A.
Transmitter and receiver

B.
Power supply

C.

Antenna

D.
Microphone

E.
Both A and D

F.
All of the above

Answer: F
Explanation:

QUESTION NO: 113

The frequency range best suited for a wireless microphone because it provides better security and lower interference is:

A.
25-50 mHz

B.
88-104 mHz

C.
88-120 mHz

D.
150-174 mHz

E.
None of the above

Answer: E
Explanation:

QUESTION NO: 114

The control software of a private board exchange (PBX) can be accessed and compromised by calling the telephone number of a device on the PBX from a computer and modem. The name of this PBX device is the:

A.
Internal and remote signal port

B.
Current carrier signaling port

C.
Time domain reflectometer

D.
Remote maintenance access terminal

E.
None of the above

Answer: D
Explanation:

QUESTION NO: 115

Which of the following is not true regarding electronic eavesdropping?

A.
An effective countermeasure to detect evidence of electronic eavesdropping in telephone equipment should be conducted by a person who is technically familiar with such equipment.

B.
An effective countermeasure would be to conduct a physical search as well as an electronic search.

C.
All wiring should be traced and accounted for.

D.
A listening device installed in a wire will cause a crackling sound, click, or other noise that can be heard on the line.

E.
None of the above.

Answer: D

Explanation:

QUESTION NO: 116

The first federal legislation that attempted to regulate electronic surveillance in the United States was enacted by Congress in:

A.
1910

B.
1924

C.
1934

D.
1968

E.
1971

Answer: C
Explanation:

QUESTION NO: 117

The manufacture, distribution, possession, and advertising of wire or oral communication interception devices is prohibited by:

A.
The First Amendment

B.
The Fourth Amendment

C.
The Federal Communications Act of 1934

D.
The Omnibus Crime Control and Safe Streets Act of 1968

E.
The FBI

Answer: D
Explanation:

QUESTION NO: 118

The criminal punishment for violation of the wiretapping phases of the Omnibus Crime Control and Safe Streets Act of 1968 is:

A.
A $10,000 fine

B.
6 months in jail and/or a $5000 fine

C.
1 year in jail and/or a $10,000 fine

D.
5 years in prison and/or a $10,000 fine

E.
None of the above

Answer: D
Explanation:

QUESTION NO: 119

Which of the following is not a requirement under the Omnibus Crime Control and Safe Streets Act of 1968 before a court may give permission for an electronic surveillance?

A.
The identity of the offender should be stated.

B.
The crime must be any felony under federal law.

C.
The place and location of the electronic surveillance must be stated.

D.
Initial approval must be granted by the attorney general of the United States or by a specially designated attorney general.

E.
All of the above.

Answer: B
Explanation:

QUESTION NO: 120

Which of the following is provided for by the Omnibus Crime Control and Safe Streets Act of 1968?

A.
It prohibits wiretapping or bugging unless a party to the intercepted conversation gives consent.

B.
It prohibits the manufacture and distribution of oral communication interceptor devices.

C.
Nonfederal law enforcement representatives are denied the right to make use of electronic surveillance unless there is a state statute permitting it.

D.
Both A and B.

E.
All of the above.

Answer: E
Explanation:

QUESTION NO: 121

Title III of the Omnibus Crime Control and Safe Streets Act of 1968 requires that an approval for electronic surveillance must be obtained from the:

A.
Chief Justice of the Supreme Court

B.
Director of the FBI

C.
Attorney general of the United States or any specially designated assistant attorney general

D.
Director of the CIA

E.
All of the above

Answer: C
Explanation:

QUESTION NO: 122

Criminal violations involving theft of trade secrets could be covered by:

A.
Theft of trade secrets statutes

B.
Bribery statutes involving trade secrets

C.
Receipt of stolen property statutes

D.
Criminal conspiracy statutes

E.
All of the above

Answer: E
Explanation:

QUESTION NO: 123

The public statute passed to protect personal information in possession of federal agencies is:

A.
The Espionage Statute

B.
The Unauthorized Disclosure Act

C.
The Omnibus Crime Control Act

D.
The Privacy Act of 1974

E.
None of the above

Answer: D
Explanation:

QUESTION NO: 124

The Privacy Act of 1974 provides which of the following safeguards?

A.
Permits individuals to gain access to certain information pertaining to themselves in federal agency records

B.
Permits individuals to determine what records pertaining to themselves are collected and maintained by federal agencies

C.
Permits individuals to prevent certain records pertaining to themselves from being used or made available for another purpose without their consent

D.
Requires federal agencies to be subject to civil suits for any damages that may occur as a result of willful or intentional action that violates an individual's rights under the Privacy Act of 1974

E.
All of the above

Answer: E
Explanation:

QUESTION NO: 125

Which of the following would not be permitted to review a student's record according to the Family Educational Rights and the Privacy Act of 1974?

A.
Law enforcement officials

B.
Other school officials

C.
The school's registrar office

D.
All of the above

E.
None of the above

Answer: A
Explanation:

QUESTION NO: 126

Which of the following characteristics pertains to a good information management program?

A.
An employee education program for those who utilize the classification system

B.
Limited number of individuals who can initiate classification of information

C.
Limitation of the duration during which the classification will remain in effect

D.
All of the above

E.
None of the above

Answer: D
Explanation:

QUESTION NO: 127

What are the three most common methods of information loss to be guarded against?

A.
Newspaper articles, magazine articles, television

B.
Employee payroll, personnel matters, market surveys

C.
Theft by an insider, inadvertent disclosure, industrial espionage

D.
Employee hirings, magazine articles, industrial espionage

E.
None of the above

Answer: C
Explanation:

QUESTION NO: 128

The elements of an information security program include:

A.
Informing employees that the information is to be protected

B.
Establishing the use of patent or nondisclosure agreements

C.
Designation of certain information as sensitive

D.
Providing the means for employees to protect sensitive information

E.
All of the above

Answer: E
Explanation:

QUESTION NO: 129

Which of the following statements is not true in regard to an information security program?

A.
The information security program is an attempt to make theft of sensitive information difficult, not necessarily to eliminate it.

B.
The protection afforded against losses by either internal or external sources is, at best, limited.

C.
A good information security program will provide total protection from industrial espionage.

D.
A trust relationship must be established and maintained with employees.

E.
The good will and compliance of employees is crucial for success.

Answer: C
Explanation:

QUESTION NO: 130

Vital records normally constitute what percentage of the company's total records?

A.
2 percent

B.
5 percent

C.
10 percent

D.
15 percent

E.
20 percent

Answer: A
Explanation:

QUESTION NO: 131

Which of the following is considered to be an approved method of protecting vital records?

A.
On-site storage in vaults or safes

B.
Protection of original vital records

C.
Natural dispersal within an outside organization

D.
Planned dispersal of copies of vital records

E.
All of the above

Answer: E
Explanation:

QUESTION NO: 132

The term "social engineering" is:

A.
A function of the personnel department in which like persons are teamed together in workshops or seminars for maximum productivity

B.
The subtle elicitation of information without revealing the true purpose of the call

C.
The specific design of a business structure to facilitate the interaction of the inhabitants

D.
Both A and C

E.
None of the above

Answer: B
Explanation:

QUESTION NO: 133

Competitive intelligence gathering is a legitimate activity that is engaged in by many firms throughout the world. The most important function of competitive intelligence is to:

A.
Alert senior management to changes in protocol in foreign countries

B.
Alert senior management as to the personal habits of competitive

C.
senior management

D.
Alert government intelligence agencies to marketplace changes

E.
Alert senior management to marketplace changes in order to prevent surprise

F.
All of the above

Answer: D
Explanation:

QUESTION NO: 134

The Secretary of Defense is not authorized to act on behalf of the following agency or department in rendering industrial security services:

A.
Department of Commerce

B.
Central Intelligence Agency

C.
Department of Justice

D.
Department of Labor

E.
None of the above

Answer: B
Explanation:

QUESTION NO: 135

The overall policy guidance for the Defense Industrial Security Program is provided by:

A.
The Federal Bureau of Investigation

B.
The Deputy Undersecretary of Defense for Policy

C.
The Assistant Chief of Staff in Intelligence

D.
The Defense Intelligence Agency

E.
None of the above

Answer: B
Explanation:

QUESTION NO: 136

The Defense Industrial Security Program on behalf of all user agencies is administered by the:

A.
Director, Defense Investigative Service

B.
Comptroller, Assistant Secretary of Defense

C.
Deputy Undersecretary of Defense for Policy

D.
Defense Industrial Security Clearance Office

E.
None of the above

Answer: A
Explanation:

QUESTION NO: 137

The executive order that applies to classified information is:

A.
E.O. 1044

B.
E.O. 1066

C.
E.O. 12065

D.
E.O. 12523

E.
E.O. 14084

Answer: C

Explanation:

QUESTION NO: 138

A controlled area established to safeguard classified material that, because of its size or nature, cannot be adequately protected by other prescribed safeguards is termed to be:

A.
A restricted area

B.
A classified area

C.
A closed area

D.
A limited area

E.
None of the above

Answer: C
Explanation:

QUESTION NO: 139

The DIS regional office under the support of the director of industrial security that has jurisdiction over the geographical area in which a facility is located is called the:

A.
Regional Security Office

B.
Division Security Office

C.
Clearance Office

D.
Cognizant Security Office

E.
None of the above

Answer: D
Explanation:

QUESTION NO: 140

Technical and intelligence information derived from foreign communications by other than the intended recipient is known as:

A.
Restricted data

B.
Communications intelligence

C.
Classified security matters

D.
Highly confidential

E.
None of the above

Answer: B
Explanation:

QUESTION NO: 141

The designation that should be applied to information or material showing unauthorized disclosure that could reasonably be expected to cause damage to national security is:

A.
Restricted

B.
Top secret

C.

Confidential

D.
Unauthorized disclosure

E.
None of the above

Answer: C
Explanation:

QUESTION NO: 142

Technical information used for training, maintenance, and inspection of classified military munitions of war would be classified as:

A.
Restricted

B.
Classified

C.
Top secret

D.
Confidential

E.
Cosmic

Answer: D
Explanation:

QUESTION NO: 143

A designation or marking that identifies classified operational keying material and that indicates the material requiring special consideration with respect to access, storage, and handling is:

A.
Cosmic

B.
Special

C.
Crypto

D.
Communications intelligence

E.
Red flagged

Answer: C
Explanation:

QUESTION NO: 144

The portion of internal security that is concerned with the protection of classified information in the hands of U.S. industry is called:

A.
Information security

B.
Classified security

C.
National security

D.
Industrial security

E.
Communications security

Answer: D
Explanation:

QUESTION NO: 145

The result of any system of administrative policies and procedures for identifying, controlling, and protecting from unauthorized disclosure of information and is authorized by executive order or statute is called:

A.
Computer security

B.
Industrial security

C.
Personnel security

D.
Communications security

E.
Information security

Answer: E
Explanation:

QUESTION NO: 146

An administrative determination that an individual is eligible for access to classified information is:

A.
Personnel security clearance

B.
Industrial security clearance

C.
National security clearance

D.
Communications security clearance

E.
None of the above

Answer: A
Explanation:

QUESTION NO: 147

The combinations to safes, containers, and vaults should be changed at intervals of:

A.
Every three months

B.
Every four months

C.
Every six months

D.
Every nine months

E.
Every year

Answer: E
Explanation:

QUESTION NO: 148

The designation that shall be applied only to information or material that unauthorized disclosure could reasonably be expected to cause serious damage to national security is:

A.
Restricted

B.
Secret

C.
Confidential

D.
Top secret

E.
Unauthorized disclosure

Answer: B
Explanation:

QUESTION NO: 149

Information regarding the revelation of significant military plans or intelligence operations should be classified as:

A.
Restricted

B.
Secret

C.
Confidential

D.
Top secret

E.
Cosmic

Answer: B
Explanation:

QUESTION NO: 150

The designation that should only be applied to information or material that unauthorized disclosure could reasonably be expected to cause exceptionally grave damage to national security is:

A.
Restricted

B.
Secret

C.
Confidential

D.
Top secret

E.
Cosmic

Answer: D
Explanation:

QUESTION NO: 151

Information that could lead to the compromise of vital national defense plans or complex cryptologic and communications intelligence systems should be classified:

A.
Restricted

B.
Secret

C.
Confidential

D.
Top secret

E.
Cosmic

Answer: D
Explanation:

QUESTION NO: 152

Regulations of the Department of Defense require that the contractor shall establish such procedures as are necessary to ensure that any employee discovering the loss, compromise, or suspected compromise of classified information outside a facility promptly reports to:

A.
The Defense Intelligence Agency

B.
The Defense Industrial Security Clearance Office

C.
The nearest FBI office

D.
Comptroller, Assistant Security of Defense

E.
The Industrial Security Office

Answer: C
Explanation:

QUESTION NO: 153

Defense Department regulations require the identification card of a defense contractor to include a:

A.
Distinctive color coding

B.
Thumbprint

C.
Photograph of the holder

D.
Symbol code

E.
All of the above

Answer: C
Explanation:

QUESTION NO: 154

Which of the following should definitely not appear on the identification card of employees of defense contractors?

A.
Distinctive color coding

B.

Symbol code

C.
Top secret, or secret

D.
Confidential

E.
Both C and D

F.
All of the above

Answer: E
Explanation:

QUESTION NO: 155

No invitation, written or oral, shall be given to a foreign national or to a representative of a foreign interest to attend any session of a meeting sponsored by a Department of Defense activity until:

A.
A full field investigation has resulted in the necessary security clearance

B.
Approval for attendance has been received from the sponsoring activity

C.
The Department of the State has given approval

D.
The CIA has given approval E. None of the above

Answer: B
Explanation:

QUESTION NO: 156

The basic document for conveying to the contractor the classification and declassification specifications for a classified contract is:

A.
DD Form 254

B.
DD Form 441

C.
DD Form 482

D.
DD Form 562

E.
DD Form 1541

Answer: A
Explanation:

QUESTION NO: 157

A document that is classified "confidential" shall exhibit the marking at:

A.
The top of the page

B.
The bottom of the page

C.
The right-hand side of the page

D.
The left-hand side of the page

E.
Both the top and bottom of the page

Answer: E
Explanation:

QUESTION NO: 158

Unclassified material should be marked:

A.
"Unclassified" at the top of the page

B.
"Unclassified" at the bottom of the page

C.
"Unclassified" at the top and bottom of the page

D.
"Unclassified" anywhere on the page

E.
With no marking

Answer: E
Explanation:

QUESTION NO: 159

An unclassified document that is attached to a classified document should have a notation stating:

A.
"Classified same as enclosure"

B.
"Treat as classified"

C.
"Unclassified when separated from classified enclosure"

D.
No notation needed

E.
None of the above

Answer: C
Explanation:

QUESTION NO: 160

Whenever classified information is downgraded, declassified, or upgraded, the material shall be promptly and conspicuously marked to indicate:

A.
What was changed

B.
The date it was changed

C.
The identity of the person taking the action

D.
All of the above

E.
None of the above

Answer: D
Explanation:

QUESTION NO: 161

Foreign classified material should be marked in accordance with instructions received from:

A.
The Defense Intelligence Agency

B.
The foreign contracting authority

C.
The FBI

D.
The Industrial Security Office

E.
None of the above

Answer: B
Explanation:

QUESTION NO: 162

Department of Defense regulations regarding the protection of classified information requires that defense contractors maintain accountability of top secret information for a minimum time of:

A.
One year

B.
Two years

C.
Three years

D.
Four years

E.
Five years

Answer: C
Explanation:

QUESTION NO: 163

When not in use, top secret information should be stored in a:

A.
Class A vault

B.
Class B vault

C.
Class C vault

D.
Class D vault

E.
Class E vault

Answer: A
Explanation:

QUESTION NO: 164

Which of the following is prohibited by the Department of Defense regulations regarding the method of transmitting top secret information outside a facility?

A.
Electronic means in a crypto system

B.
Armed Forces Courier Service

C.
Designated courier that has been cleared

D.
U.S. Postal Service

E.
Specifically designated escort

Answer: D
Explanation:

QUESTION NO: 165

Secret information can be transmitted by which of the following means according to Department of Defense regulations?

A.
Designated courier that has been cleared

B.
U.S. Registered Mail

C.
Armed Forces Courier Service

D.
Both A and C

E.
All of the above

Answer: E
Explanation:

QUESTION NO: 166

Department of Defense regulations indicate that destruction of classified information can be accomplished by:

A.
Melting

B.
Burning

C.
Mutilation

D.
Chemical decomposition

E.
All of the above

Answer: E
Explanation:

QUESTION NO: 167

Which of the following has the appropriate security clearances in the destruction of top secret and secret information according to Department of Defense regulations?

A.
Two employees of the defense contractor

B.
Three employees of the defense contractor

C.

Four employees of the defense contractor

D.
One employee of the Department of Defense and two employees of the defense contractor

E.
None of the above

Answer: A
Explanation:

QUESTION NO: 168

According to Department of Defense regulations, if classified material is removed from the facility for destruction, it should be destroyed:

A.
The same day it was removed

B.
Within two days

C.
Within three days

D.
Within one week

E.
Within ten days

Answer: A
Explanation:

QUESTION NO: 169

According to Department of Defense regulations, to be eligible for a personnel security clearance for confidential information, the following age must be attained:

A.

16

B.
18

C.
20

D.
21

E.
25

Answer: A
Explanation:

QUESTION NO: 170

According to Department of Defense regulations, the security clearance of a contractual employee shall be effective for:

A.
Six months

B.
One year

C.
Two years

D.
Five years

E.
For as long as he or she is employed by the contractor

Answer: E
Explanation:

QUESTION NO: 171

According to Department of Defense regulations, the following are not eligible for a personnel security clearance:

A.
All foreign nationals

B.
All foreign nationals except those granted reciprocal clearances

C.
Only foreign nationals that are from a communist country

D.
Only foreign nationals that are under 16

E.
None of the above

Answer: B
Explanation:

QUESTION NO: 172

A facility security clearance should not be granted to contractor activities:

A.
In Puerto Rico

B.
In facilities determined to be under foreign ownership, control, or influence

C.
In U.S. trust territories

D.
Both A and C

E.
All of the above

Answer: B
Explanation:

QUESTION NO: 173

For personnel security clearances required in connection with a facility security clearance, applications shall be submitted to the:

A.
Defense Intelligence Agency

B.
Industrial Clearance Office

C.
Contracting officer

D.
Cognizant Security Office

E.
Central Intelligence Agency

Answer: D
Explanation:

QUESTION NO: 174

According to Department of Defense regulations, "interim" personnel security clearances must be approved by the:

A.
Defense Intelligence Agency

B.
Industrial Clearance Office

C.
Contracting officer

D.
Cognizant Security Office

E.
None of the above

Answer: C
Explanation:

QUESTION NO: 175

Department of Defense regulations require initial approval in writing prior to processing any classified information in an ADP system by which of the following authorities:

A.
The head of the Industrial Security Clearance Office

B.
National Security Agency

C.
Cognizant Security Office

D.
The contracting officer

E.
Defense Intelligence Agency

Answer: C
Explanation:

QUESTION NO: 176

An ADP system that operates in a manner where all users with access to the system have both a security clearance and a need to-know status for all classified information that is in the system is known as:

A.
Classified Security Mode

B.
Restricted Security Mode

C.
Controlled Security Mode

D.
Dedicated Security Mode

E.
Limited Security Mode

Answer: D
Explanation:

QUESTION NO: 177

An ADP system that operates in a manner in which all users with access to the system who have a security clearance for the highest classification and most restrictive types of information in the system is known as:

A.
Classified Security Mode

B.
Restricted Security Mode

C.
Controlled Security Mode

D.
System High Security Mode

E.
Dedicated Security Mode

Answer: D
Explanation:

QUESTION NO: 178

An ADP system that operates in a manner in which at least some of the users with access to the system have neither a security clearance nor a need-to-know status for all classified information that is in the system, but in a manner that the cognizant security officer or a higher authority has determined that the necessary degree of security has been achieved and maintained, is known as:

A.
Limited Security Mode

B.
Classified Security Mode

C.
Controlled Security Mode

D.
Restricted Security Mode

E.
Dedicated Security Mode

Answer: C
Explanation:

QUESTION NO: 179

The ADP system security supervisor or designee should review the audit trail logs at least:

A.
Daily

B.
Weekly

C.
Monthly

D.
Bimonthly

E.
Quarterly

Answer: B
Explanation:

QUESTION NO: 180

The Department of Defense Personnel Security Questionnaire (Industrial) Form is:

A.
DD 16

B.
DD 48

C.
DD 254

D.
DD 441

E.
DD 482

Answer: B
Explanation:

QUESTION NO: 181

According to Department of Defense regulations, which of the following documents are not acceptable proof of U.S. citizenship concerning the safeguarding of classified information?

A.
Birth certificate

B.
Certificate of naturalization

C.
Certificate of citizenship

D.
Uncertified copy of baptismal record

E.
All of the above

Answer: D
Explanation:

QUESTION NO: 182

Of the following substance schedules, which has no current accepted medical use?

A.
Schedule I

B.
Schedule II

C.
Schedule III

D.
Schedule IV

E.
Schedule V

Answer: A
Explanation:

QUESTION NO: 183

Of the following substance schedules, which one has an accepted medical use in treatment and a high potential for abuse that could lead to severe psychological and physical dependence?

A.
Schedule I

B.
Schedule II

C.
Schedule III

D.
Schedule IV

E.
Schedule V

Answer: B
Explanation:

QUESTION NO: 184

Of the following substance schedules, which one has an accepted medical use in treatment and a low potential for abuse with limited psychological and physical dependence when compared to other substances and drugs?

A.
Schedule I

B.
Schedule II

C.
Schedule III

D.
Schedule IV

E.
Schedule V

Answer: D
Explanation:

QUESTION NO: 185

The Controlled Substances Act has imposed certain record-keeping requirements on those involved in the manufacturing, purchasing, and distribution of substances under the Act. Which of the following is not one of the specific requirements?

A.
Record-keeping requirements apply to all substances under control, regardless of schedule.

B.
Record-keeping requirements state that full records be kept of all quantities that are manufactured, purchased, sold, and inventoried of the substance by each handler.

C.

Records for Schedule I and Schedule II drugs must be kept separate from all other records of the handler.

D.
Records for Schedule III, IV, and V drugs must be kept in a form defined as "readily available. "

E.
Record-keeping requirements only apply to Schedule I, II, and III substances.

Answer: E
Explanation:

QUESTION NO: 186

The primary federal law that provides the legal foundation for the current federal strategy of reducing the consumption of illicit drugs is:

A.
The Harrison Narcotics Act

B.
The Volstead Act

C.
Title II, Comprehensive Drug Abuse Prevention and Control Act of 1970

D.
The Drug Enforcement Administration Act of 1982

E.
None of the above

Answer: C
Explanation:

QUESTION NO: 187

Which of the following is correct in the regulatory requirements of Schedule V substances under the Controlled Substances Act?

A.

Keeping readily retrievable records

B.
Registration by those who handle or intend to handle the substance

C.
Use of a regulated storage area

D.
No written prescription is required

E.
International transactions must be made with prior notice to the DEA

F.
All of the above

Answer: F
Explanation:

QUESTION NO: 188

The Federal Act mandates that for simple possession of any controlled substance the first offense is:

A.
Up to 1 year in jail/prison and/or a $5000 fine

B.
Up to 2 years in prison and/or a $5000 fine

C.
Up to 3 years in prison and/or a $10,000 fine

D.
Up to 5 years in prison and/or a $15,000 fine

E.
Up to 15 years in prison and/or a $25,000 fine

Answer: A
Explanation:

QUESTION NO: 189

The federal trafficking penalty for a Schedule I narcotic that is the first offense is:

A.
5 years in prison and/or a $10,000 fine

B.
10 years in prison and/or a $20,000 fine

C.
15 years in prison and/or a $25,000 fine

D.
20 years in prison and/or a $30,000 fine

E.
30 years in prison and/or a $50,000 fine

Answer: C
Explanation:

QUESTION NO: 190

Which of the following is not correct regarding narcotics?

A.
They have been used for a long period of time as a remedy for diarrhea.

B.
The term "narcotic" in its medical meaning refers to opium and opium derivatives or a synthetic substitute.

C.
They tend to intensify vision and increase alertness.

D.
They are the most effective agents known for the relief of intense pain.

E.
They can cause respiratory depression in some cases.

Answer: C
Explanation:

QUESTION NO: 191

Which of the following is not designated as a narcotic?

A.
Codeine

B.
Morphine

C.
Heroin

D.
Cocaine

E.
Librium

Answer: E
Explanation:

QUESTION NO: 192

The main source of nonsynthetic narcotics is:

A.
The laboratory

B.
Poppy, Papaver somniferum

C.
The coca plant

D.
Peyote

E.
None of the above

Answer: B

Explanation:

QUESTION NO: 193

Narcotics are known by a number of trade names. One of the trade names is:

A.
Quaalude

B.
Azene

C.
Valium

D.
Paregoric

E.
Butisol

Answer: D
Explanation:

QUESTION NO: 194

Which of the following is a characteristic of morphine?

A.
It is the principal constituent of opium.

B.
Its legal use is restricted primarily to hospitals.

C.
It is odorless, bitter tasting, and darkens with age.

D.
Only a small part of the morphine obtained from opium is used medically.

E.
Both A and D

F.
All of the above.

Answer: F
Explanation:

QUESTION NO: 195

Which naturally occurring narcotic is by far the most widely used, and is often combined with other products such as aspirin or Tylenol?

A.
Methadone

B.
Codeine

C.
Barbiturates

D.
Chloral hydrate

E.
None of the above

Answer: B
Explanation:

QUESTION NO: 196

Watery eyes, runny, nose, yawning, loss of appetite, irritability, tremors, panic, chills and sweating, cramps, and nausea would indicate withdrawal symptoms of:

A.
Barbiturates

B.
Stimulants

C.

Heroin

D.
Cocaine

E.
LSD

Answer: C
Explanation:

QUESTION NO: 197

Which of the following is a correct statement pertaining to heroin?

A.
The first comprehensive control of heroin in the United States was established with the Harrison Narcotic Act of 1914.

B.
Pure heroin is rarely sold on the street.

C.
The Bayer Company in Germany first started commercial production of heroin as a pain remedy in the latter part of the nineteenth century.

D.
Pure heroin is a white powder and is also known as "horse."

E.
Both B and D.

F.
All of the above.

Answer: F
Explanation:

QUESTION NO: 198

Which of the following does not apply to synthetic narcotics?

A.
Two of the most widely available synthetic narcotics are meperidine and methadone.

B.
Synthetic narcotics are produced entirely within the laboratory.

C.
Synthetic narcotics are also covered by the Controlled Substances Act.

D.
Meperidine can be administered by injection or taken orally.

E.
Large doses can result in convulsions.

F.
None of the above.

Answer: F
Explanation:

QUESTION NO: 199

Which of the following is not a correct statement regarding methadone?

A.
Methadone was synthesized in Germany during World War II because of a shortage of morphine.

B.
Methadone was introduced to the United States in 1947 and was distributed under such names as amidone, dolophine, and methadone.

C.
Methadone is chemically like morphine and heroin.

D.
Methadone was widely used in the 1960s in the treatment of narcotic addicts.

E.
Methadone is only effective when administered by injection.

F.
Both C and E.

Answer: F

Explanation:

QUESTION NO: 200

Which of the following drugs is classified as a "depressant" under the Controlled Substances Act?

A.
Morphine

B.
Cocaine

C.
Phenmetrazine

D.
Methaqualone

E.
None of the above

Answer: D
Explanation:

QUESTION NO: 201

Cold and clammy skin, dilated pupils, shallow breathing, and 2. weak and rapid pulse are overdose symptoms resulting from which of the following substances?

A.
Cocaine

B.
Barbiturates

C.
Methylphenidate

D.
Heroin

E.

LSD

Answer: B
Explanation:

QUESTION NO: 202

Which of the following is not correct pertaining to the use of depressants?

A.
Excessive use results in drunken behavior similar to that of alcohol.

B.
Taken as prescribed, they are beneficial for relief of tension and anxiety.

C.
Taken in low doses, they will produce mild sedation.

D.
The intoxicating effects of depressants are the same as narcotics.

E.
Depressants can be used as a means of suicide.

Answer: D
Explanation:

QUESTION NO: 203

Which of the following substances would be classified as a depressant under the Controlled Substance Act?

A.
Preludin

B.
Darvon

C.
Miltown

D.
Dilaudid

E.
Pethadol

F.
All of the above

Answer: C
Explanation:

QUESTION NO: 204

Depressants of various types are included in Schedules II, III, and IV of the Controlled Substances Act. Which of the following does not apply to the use of depressants?

A.
Depressants have a high potential for abuse.

B.
Some drug abusers often resort to the use of depressants to soothe their nerves after the use of stimulants.

C.
The use of depressants compounded with alcohol can cause death.

D.
Moderate depressant poisoning closely resembles intoxication from alcohol.

E.
One of the recognized features from the use of depressants is that tolerance will not develop.

Answer: E
Explanation:

QUESTION NO: 205

Which of the following withdrawal characteristics can result from the abrupt cessation or reduction of high-dose depressant usage?

A.
The withdrawal symptoms associated with depressants are more serious than those of any other drugs of abuse.

B.
Convulsions can be experienced that are indistinguishable from those occurring in grand mal epilepsy.

C.
Detoxification and treatment must be carried out under close medical supervision.

D.
Both A and C.

E.
All of the above.

Answer: E
Explanation:

QUESTION NO: 206

Which of the following is not a correct statement regarding chloral hydrate?

A.
It is the oldest of the sleep-inducing drugs, also known as hypnotic drugs.

B.
It is a liquid marketed in the form of syrups and soft gelatin capsules.

C.
Its popularity decreased after the introduction of barbiturates.

D.
Its main abuse is by young adults.

E.
It has a bitter caustic taste and a slightly acrid odor.

Answer: D
Explanation:

QUESTION NO: 207

Which of the following characteristics describes barbiturates?

A.
They are used by both physicians and veterinarians to induce sedation and sleep.

B.
Larger doses cause sleep 20 to 60 minutes after oral administration.

C.
Some individuals may experience a sense of excitement before sedation takes effect.

D.
Barbiturates are classified as ultra-short, short, intermediate, and long-acting.

E.
All of the above.

F.
None of the above.

Answer: E
Explanation:

QUESTION NO: 208

Barbiturates have about 2500 derivatives of barbituric acid and are known by a variety of names. Which of the following is another name for a barbiturate?

A.
Demerol

B.
Pethadol

C.
Leritine

D.
Butisol

E.
Talwin

F.

All of the above

Answer: D
Explanation:

QUESTION NO: 209

Which of the following is not another name for a barbiturate?

A.
Tuinal

B.
Butisol

C.
Phenobarbital

D.
Amobarbital

E.
Dilaudid

F.
None of the above

Answer: E
Explanation:

QUESTION NO: 210

Which of the following identifies the depressant methaqualone?

A.
It was once mistakenly thought to be effective as an aphrodisiac.

B.
It is administered orally.

C.

It is a Schedule I drug in the Controlled Substances Act.

D.
It is chemically unrelated to the barbiturates.

E.
It is also known as Quaalude.

F.
All of the above.

Answer: F
Explanation:

QUESTION NO: 211

Which of the following is not another name for methaqualone?

A.
Optimil

B.
Darvon

C.
Parest

D.
Sopor

E.
Voranil

F.
Both B and E

Answer: F
Explanation:

QUESTION NO: 212

Which of the following describes meprobamate?

A.
It was first synthesized in 1950.

B.
It is primarily prescribed for the relief of anxiety and tension as well as muscle spasms.

C.
It does not produce sleep at therapeutic doses.

D.
Excessive use can result in physical and psychological dependence.

E.
All of the above.

F.
None of the above.

Answer: E
Explanation:

QUESTION NO: 213

Which of the following is not a brand name of meprobamate?

A.
Miltown

B.
Equanil

C.
Preludin

D.
SK-Bamate

E.
Kesso-Bamate

Answer: C
Explanation:

QUESTION NO: 214

Which of the following is not correct with regard to benzodiazepine?

A.
This family of depressants is used to relieve anxiety and tension.

B.
This depressant relieves muscle spasms and prevents convulsions.

C.
When used to induce a "high," this depressant is taken in combination with other substances such as alcohol or marijuana.

D.
This depressant is safer to use than that of other depressants.

E.
Excessive use may result in physical and psychological dependence.

F.
None of the above.

Answer: F
Explanation:

QUESTION NO: 215

Which of the following is a member of the benzodiazepine group known in the United States?

A.
Librium

B.
Klonopin

C.
Valium

D.
Serax

E.
All of the above

Answer: E
Explanation:

QUESTION NO: 216

Excitation, increased alertness, euphoria, increased pulse rate and blood pressure, insomnia, and loss of appetite are symptoms of:

A.
Hallucinogens

B.
Depressants

C.
Stimulants

D.
Benzodiazepines

E.
Marijuana

Answer: C
Explanation:

QUESTION NO: 217

All of the following are controlled substances grouped as stimulants except:

A.
Cocaine

B.
Methyphenidate

C.
Mescaline

D.
Amphetamines

E.
Phenmetrazine

Answer: C
Explanation:

QUESTION NO: 218

Which of the following characteristics describes stimulants as a controlled substance?

A.
Younger individuals who use stimulants for a euphoric effect often go on to experiment with other drugs of abuse.

B.
Users tend to rely on stimulants to feel stronger, more decisive and self-possessed.

C.
Stimulants are usually administered by injection or taken orally.

D.
Heavy use could result in psychological dependence.

E.
Tolerance develops from heavy use.

F.
All of the above.

Answer: F
Explanation:

QUESTION NO: 219

Which of the following is not known as a stimulant?

A.
Cocaine

B.
Doriden

C.
Ritalin

D.
Bacarate

E.
Preludin

Answer: E
Explanation:

QUESTION NO: 220

Cocaine is derived from which of the following?

A.
Cactus plant

B.
Poppy plant

C.
Coffee bean

D.
Coca plant

E.
Mushrooms

Answer: D
Explanation:

QUESTION NO: 221

Which of the following is a correct statement regarding illicit cocaine?

A.
It is very popular as a recreational drug.

B.
It has the potential for extraordinary psychic dependency due to its pleasurable effect.

C.
It is distributed as a white crystalline powder and is also known as snow.

D.
It is often adulterated to about half its volume by a variety of other ingredients.

E.
It is commonly administered by snorting through the nasal passages.

F.
All of the above

Answer: F
Explanation:

QUESTION NO: 222

Cocaine is placed in which of the following controlled substance schedules?

A.
Schedule I

B.
Schedule II

C.
Schedule III

D.
Schedule IV

E.
Schedule V

Answer: B
Explanation:

QUESTION NO: 223

Which of the following is not known as an amphetamine?

A.
Biphetamine

B.
Delcobese

C.
Desoxyn

D.
Dexedrine

E.
None of the above

Answer: E
Explanation:

QUESTION NO: 224

Which of the following substances would induce poor perception of time and distance?

A.
Stimulants

B.
Depressants

C.
Hallucinogens

D.
Cannabis

E.
Narcotics

Answer: C
Explanation:

QUESTION NO: 225

Which of the following does not describe hallucinogens?

A.
Pupils are dilated with a rise in body temperature and blood pressure.

B.
They induce a state of excitation of the central nervous system.

C.
They are Schedule III substances.

D.
Long after hallucinogens are eliminated from the body, users may experience "flashbacks."

E.
Suicide can sometimes result from severe depression after use.

Answer: E
Explanation:

QUESTION NO: 226

Which one of the following substances is not a hallucinogen?

A.
Lysergic acid diethylamide

B.
Mescaline

C.
Phencyclidine

D.
Phencyclidine analogs

E.
None of the above

Answer: E
Explanation:

QUESTION NO: 227

The hallucinogen mescaline is derived from:

A.
The coca plant

B.
The sage bush

C.
The peyote cactus

D.
Mushrooms

E.
Dandelions

Answer: C
Explanation:

QUESTION NO: 228

Which of the following statements is correct regarding LSD?

A.
It is produced from lysergic acid, which is a substance derived from the ergot fungus that grows on rye.

B.
Its psychotomimetic effects were discovered accidentally.

C.
Its popularity declined after the 1960s.

D.
Tolerance develops rapidly

E.
All of the above.

Answer: E
Explanation:

QUESTION NO: 229

According to a consensus of drug treatment professionals, the drug that now poses a greater risk to the user than any other drug of abuse is:

A.
Heroin

B.
Cocaine

C.
Phencyclidine

D.
Chloral hydrate

E.
Marijuana

Answer: C
Explanation:

QUESTION NO: 230

Which of the following is not a true statement in regard to phencyclidine?

A.
It is also known as angel dust and PCP.

B.
It is unique among popular drugs of abuse in its power to produce psychoses that are indistinguishable from schizophrenia.

C.
Most phencyclidine is produced in clandestine laboratories.

D.
It is a Schedule I substance.

E.
None of the above.

Answer: D
Explanation:

QUESTION NO: 231

Marijuana comes from:

A.
The peyote cactus

B.
The cannabis plant

C.
The poppy plant

D.
The coca plant

E.
Mushrooms

Answer: B
Explanation:

QUESTION NO: 232

Marijuana and other cannabis products are usually administered by:

A.
Sniffing

B.
Injection

C.
Rubbing into the skin

D.
Smoking

E.
"Mainstreaming"

Answer: D
Explanation:

QUESTION NO: 233

Marijuana is known by which of the following names?

A.
Reefer

B.
Acapulco Gold

C.
Grass

D.
Pot

E.
Thai sticks

F.
All of the above

Answer: F
Explanation:

QUESTION NO: 234

Hashish mainly comes from:

A.
Peru

B.
Chile

C.
Colombia

D.
South Africa

E.
The Middle East

Answer: E
Explanation:

QUESTION NO: 235

The physiological adaptation of the body to the presence of a dmg whereby the body develops a continuing need for the dmg is known as:

A.
Tolerance

B.
Addiction

C.
Psychological dependence

D.
Physical dependence

E.
Habituation

Answer: D
Explanation:

QUESTION NO: 236

The condition whereby a user must keep increasing the dosage to maintain the same effect is known as:

A.
Tolerance

B.
Addiction

C.
Psychological dependence

D.
Physical dependence

E.
Habituation

Answer: A
Explanation:

QUESTION NO: 237

The condition whereby the user of a substance develops an attachment to the dmg because of the substance's ability to satisfy some emotional or personality need of the user is known as:

A.
Tolerance

B.
Addiction

C.
Psychological dependence

D.
Physical dependence

E.
Psychosis

Answer: C
Explanation:

QUESTION NO: 238

The state of periodic or chronic intoxication produced by the repeated consumption of a substance is known as:

A.
Tolerance

B.
Addiction

C.
Dmg dependence

D.
Habituation

E.
Psychosis

Answer: B
Explanation:

QUESTION NO: 239

What process does a security manager use in establishing priorities in the protection of assets?

A.
Audit survey

B.
Security survey

C.
Risk analysis or assessment

D.
Inspection review

E.
Both B and C

F.
All of the above

Answer: E
Explanation:

QUESTION NO: 240

The degree of protection desired in any installation is predicated on an analysis of which of the following?

A.
Cost and vulnerability

B.
Cost and criticality

C.
Criticality and vulnerability

D.
Vulnerability and environmental conditions

E.
None of the above

Answer: C
Explanation:

QUESTION NO: 241

A critical on-site examination and analysis of a facility to ascertain the present security status and to identify deficiencies or excesses in determining the protection needed to make recommendations to improve overall security is the definition of a(n):

A.
Full-field inspection

B.
Inspection review

C.
Audit survey

D.

Security survey

E.
None of the above

Answer: D
Explanation:

QUESTION NO: 242

What is a key consideration in a risk analysis or risk assessment process?

A.
Vulnerability to attack

B.
Probability of attack

C.
Cost

D.
Impact to the business if loss occurs

E.
Both A and B

F.
All of the above

Answer: F
Explanation:

QUESTION NO: 243

From a security perspective, what is the first factor to be considered in facility construction?

A.
The identity of experienced consultants

B.

An effective security plan

C.
The building site itself

D.
An architect with knowledge of physical security

E.
None of the above

Answer: C
Explanation:

QUESTION NO: 244

Which of the following is not correct regarding a security education program?

A.
Many people are naive and trusting.

B.
All installation personnel must be made aware of the constant threat of breaches of security.

C.
Structural aids to security are valueless without active support of all personnel.

D.
Security consciousness is an inherent state of mind.

E.
None of the above.

Answer: D
Explanation:

QUESTION NO: 245

The most vulnerable link in any identification system is:

A.

Poor quality of identification badges

B.
Educational background of security officers

C.
Not enough security officers assigned to control posts

D.
Identification cards are too small

E.
Perfunctory performance of duty

F.
None of the above

Answer: E
Explanation:

QUESTION NO: 246

Which of the following is not true in regard to establishing and identifying personnel to control movement?

A.
The identification card should be designed as simply as possible.

B.
Detailed instructions should be disseminated as to where, when, and how badges should be worn.

C.
Procedures should be designed to show employees what to do when an identification card or badge is lost.

D.
The identification card or badge should be designed in a relatively complicated manner to avoid duplication.

E.
Prerequisites should be devised and disseminated for reissue.

Answer: D
Explanation:

QUESTION NO: 247

The use of a simple codeword or phrase during a normal conversation to alert other security personnel that an authorized person has been forced to vouch for an unauthorized individual is termed:

A.
Code one

B.
SOS

C.
Security alert

D.
Duress code

E.
Basic alert

Answer: D
Explanation:

QUESTION NO: 248

The practice of having at least two authorized persons, each capable of detecting incorrect or unauthorized procedures with respect to the task being performed, present during any operation that affords access to a sensitive area is referred to as a(n):

A.
Two-man access procedure

B.
Two-man control rule

C.
Two-man rule

D.
Controlled access rule

E.

Information security rule

F.
None of the above

Answer: C
Explanation:

QUESTION NO: 249

The designation and establishment of "restricted areas" according to army regulations is performed by the:

A.
Joint Chiefs of Staff

B.
National Security Agency

C.
The Secretary of Defense

D.
The Secretary of the Army

E.
The military commander of the installation or facility

Answer: E
Explanation:

QUESTION NO: 250

Which of the following is not a known advantage of the establishment of restricted areas?

A.
They provide an increase in security without slowdown in operation.

B.
They provide increased security through buffer zones.

C.
They allow for varying degrees of security as required.

D.
They improve overall security.

E.
They make it possible to have security compatible with operational requirements.

Answer: A
Explanation:

QUESTION NO: 251

A restricted area containing a security interest or other sensitive matter, which uncontrolled movement can permit access to the security interest or sensitive matter, but within which access may be prevented by security escort and other internal restrictions and controls, is called a(n):

A.
Exclusion area

B.
Controlled area

C.
Limited area

D.
Sensitized area

E.
None of the above

Answer: C
Explanation:

QUESTION NO: 252

What type of fencing is generally used for protection of limited and exclusion areas?

A.

Concertina

B.
Barbed tape

C.
Barbed wire

D.
Chain-link

E.
Wood

Answer: D
Explanation:

QUESTION NO: 253

Excluding the top guard, a chain-link fence for general security purposes should be:

A.
6 gauge

B.
7 gauge

C.
8 gauge

D.
9 gauge

E.
10 gauge

Answer: D
Explanation:

QUESTION NO: 254

In a chain-link fence with mesh openings for general security purposes, the openings should be no larger than:

A.
11/5 inches

B.
2 inches

C.
2112 inches

D.
4 inches

E.
4 ½ inches

Answer: B
Explanation:

QUESTION NO: 255

Excluding the top guard, standard barbed-wire fencing that is intended to prevent human trespassing should not be less than:

A.
6 feet high

B.
7 feet high

C.
8 feet high

D.
9 feet high

E.
10 feet high

Answer: B
Explanation:

QUESTION NO: 256

The federal specification regarding standard barbed-wire fencing that is twisted and double-strand is that it should be:

A.
8 gauge

B.
10 gauge

C.
12 gauge

D.
14 gauge

E.
None of the above

Answer: C
Explanation:

QUESTION NO: 257

A standard barbed-wire, twisted, double-strand fence has __ point barbs spaced an equal distance apart.

A.
1

B.
2

C.
3

D.
4

E.
5

Answer: D
Explanation:

QUESTION NO: 258

The distance in a barbed-wire fence should not exceed:

A.
2 inches

B.
3 inches

C.
4 inches

D.
5 inches

E.
6 inches

Answer: E
Explanation:

QUESTION NO: 259

Top-guard supporting arms should be permanently affixed to the top of the fence 'posts to increase the overall height of the fence by at least:

A.
1 foot

B.
11/2 feet

C.
2 feet

D.
21/2 feet

E.
3 feet

Answer: A
Explanation:

QUESTION NO: 260

A top guard must consist of:

A.
Two strands of barbed wire or tape

B.
Three strands of barbed wire or tape

C.
Four strands of barbed wire or tape

D.
Five strands of barbed wire or tape

E.
Six strands of barbed wire or tape

Answer: B
Explanation:

QUESTION NO: 261

How many inches apa1t should strands of barbed wire or tape used as a top guard on a fence be spaced?

A.
2

B.
3

C.

4

D.
5

E.
6

Answer: E
Explanation:

QUESTION NO: 262

Unavoidable drainage ditches, culverts, vents, ducts, and other openings should be protected by securely fastened welded-bar grills when they have a cross-sectional area greater than:

A.
10 square inches

B.
48 square inches

C.
64 square inches

D.
96 square inches

E.
04 square inches

Answer: D
Explanation:

QUESTION NO: 263

Between the perimeter barrier and exterior structures should be a clear zone covering:

A.
10 feet

B.
15 feet

C.
20 feet

D.
30 feet

E.
40 feet

Answer: C
Explanation:

QUESTION NO: 264

As a general rule, between the perimeter barrier and structures within the protected area, except when a building is a part of the perimeter barrier, there should be a clear zone of at least:

A.
10 feet

B.
20 feet

C.
30 feet

D.
40 feet

E.
50 feet

Answer: E
Explanation:

QUESTION NO: 265

Manhole covers _____ inches or more in diameter should be secured to prevent unauthorized openings.

A.
10

B.
20

C.
30

D.
40

E.
50

Answer: A
Explanation:

QUESTION NO: 266

Which of the following characteristics of protective lighting is incorrect?

A.
It may be unnecessary where the perimeter fence is protected by a central alarm system.

B.
It usually requires less intensity than working light.

C.
It may also provide personal protection by reducing advantages of concealment.

D.
It should only be used as a psychological deterrent.

E.
Such lighting is expensive to maintain.

Answer: E
Explanation:

QUESTION NO: 267

Measured horizontally 6 inches above ground level and at least 30 feet outside the exclusion area to barrier, the perimeter band of lighting must provide a minimum intensity of:

A.
0.2 foot-candle

B.
0.3 foot-candle

C.
0.4 foot-candle

D.
0.6 foot-candle

E.
0.10 foot-candle

Answer: A
Explanation:

QUESTION NO: 268

Which of the following principles of protective lighting is not correct?

A.
Lighting should be used with other measures, such as fixed security posts, fences, etc., and not used alone.

B.
A large amount of light should be focused on security patrol routes.

C.
Adequate, even light should be used on bordering areas.

D.
There should be a high brightness contrast between an intruder and the background.

E.
Glaring lights should be directed at the eyes of an intruder.

Answer: B
Explanation:

QUESTION NO: 269

Lighting units of four general types are used for protective lighting. Which of the following is not used?

A.
Emergency

B.
Movable

C.
Standby

D.
Intermittent

E.
Continuous

Answer: D
Explanation:

QUESTION NO: 270

'What is the most common protective lighting system that consists of a series of fixed luminaries arranged to flood a given area during the hours of darkness with overlapping cones of light?

A.
Emergency lighting

B.
Movable lighting

C.
Standby lighting

D.
Intermittent lighting

E.
Continuous lighting

Answer: E
Explanation:

QUESTION NO: 271

Piers and docks located on an installation should be safeguarded by illuminating both water approaches and the pier area. Decks on open piers should be illuminated to at least:

A.
0.5 foot-candle

B.
1.0 foot-candle

C.
1.5 foot-candles

D.
2.0 foot-candles

E.
3.0 foot-candles

Answer: B
Explanation:

QUESTION NO: 272

Water approaches that extend to 100 feet from the pier should be illuminated to at least:

A.
0.5 foot-candle

B.
1.0 foot-candle

C.
1.5 foot-candles

D.
2.0 foot-candles

E.
3.0 foot-candles

Answer: A
Explanation:

QUESTION NO: 273

U.S. Army illumination intensity minimums for lighting the perimeter of a restricted area is:

A.
0.15 foot-candle

B.
0.40 foot-candle

C.
1.00 foot-candle

D.
2.00 foot-candles

E.
2.15 foot-candles

Answer: B
Explanation:

QUESTION NO: 274

What agency should be consulted before installing protective lighting adjacent to navigable waters?

A.
Local law enforcement agencies

B.
The Department of Transportation

C.
The Bureau of Customs

D.
The U.S. Coast Guard

E.
Both A and B

Answer: D
Explanation:

QUESTION NO: 275

The intrusion detection system in which a pattern of radio waves is transmitted and partially reflected back to the antenna is known as a(n):

A.
Capacitance detection system

B.
Ultrasonic detection system

C.
Vibration detection system

D.
Electromechanical detection system

E.
Microwave detection system

Answer: E
Explanation:

QUESTION NO: 276

The intrusion detection system that is used on safes, walls, and openings in an effort to establish an electrostatic field around an object to be protected is known as a(n):

A.

Capacitance detection system

B.
Ultrasonic detection system

C.
Contact microphone detection system

D.
Microwave detection system

E.
Radio frequency detection system

Answer: A
Explanation:

QUESTION NO: 277

An alarm system in which the installation-owned system is a direct extension of the police or fire alarm system is known as a(n):

A.
Central station system

B.
Local alarm system

C.
Proprietary system

D.
Auxiliary system

E.
Bell-sound system

Answer: D
Explanation:

QUESTION NO: 278

An alarm system that is monitored by an outside company to provide electric protective services in which they provide the appropriate actions is known as a(n):

A.
Central station system

B.
Local alarm system

C.
Proprietary system

D.
Auxiliary system

E.
Bell-sound system

Answer: A
Explanation:

QUESTION NO: 279

An alarm system whereby the central station is owned by and located within the installation being protected is known as a(n):

A.
Central station system

B.
Local alarm system

C.
Proprietary system

D.
Auxiliary system

E.
Bell-sound system

Answer: C
Explanation:

QUESTION NO: 280

The principle of the pin-tumbler lock can be traced back historically to:

A.
Egyptians more than 4000 years ago

B.
The Civil War period

C.
The late eighteenth century

D.
1905

E.
World War I

Answer: A
Explanation:

QUESTION NO: 281

Which of the following is not true with regard to lock and key systems?

A.
The locking system should be supplemented with other security devices.

B.
Most key locks can be picked by an expert in a few minutes.

C.
A high-quality pickproof lock is considered a positive bar to entry.

D.
The lock is the most accepted and widely used security device of the basic safeguards in protecting installations.

E.
Locks, regardless of quality or cost, should be considered as delay devices only.

Answer: C
Explanation:

QUESTION NO: 282

Of the following locks, which one type is generally considered to have the poorest security value?

A.
An interchangeable core system

B.
Conventional combination locks

C.
Key locks

D.
Manipulation-resistant combination locks

E.
Both A and D

F.
None of the above

Answer: C
Explanation:

QUESTION NO: 283

The number of combinations possible with a lock that has 40 numbers and a 3-number combination is:

A.
12,000

B.
16,000

C.
32,000

D.
64,000

E.
86,000

Answer: D
Explanation:

QUESTION NO: 284

Which lock is generally used on automobiles, desks, and cabinets?

A.
Wafer

B.
Ward

C.
Pin tumbler

D.
Combination

E.
Cypher

Answer: A
Explanation:

QUESTION NO: 285

Which of the following is not true with regard to door latches?

A.
A dead-bolt latch is easy to install and can be used on almost any door.

B.
Chain latches are highly recommended as effective security measures.

C.
A dead-bolt latch is very expensive.

D.
A dead-bolt latch increases the security posture of the facility.

E.
Both B and C

F.
Both A and D

Answer: E
Explanation:

QUESTION NO: 286

An inventory of key systems should be conducted at least:

A.
Weekly

B.
Monthly

C.
Quarterly

D.
Semiannually

E.
Annually

Answer: E
Explanation:

QUESTION NO: 287

A sentry dog normally does not perform as well at:

A.
Radar sites

B.
Warehouses

C.
Gasoline storage areas

D.
Ammunition storage areas

E.
Offices containing classified materials

Answer: C
Explanation:

QUESTION NO: 288

Which of the following is more of a probable disadvantage in the use of sentry dogs?

A.
A dog is more effective than a human during inclement weather.

B.
A dog has a keen sense of smell.

C.
A dog provides a strong psychological deterrent.

D.
The type of dog best suited for security work is naturally dangerous.

E.
A dog can detect and apprehend intruders.

Answer: D
Explanation:

QUESTION NO: 289

In meeting federal specifications, insulated units must have the following fire-resistant minimum ratings:

A.
Class 150: two hours

B.
Class 150: four hours

C.
Class 350: one hour

D.
Class 350: three hours

E.
Class 350: four hours

Answer: C
Explanation:

QUESTION NO: 290

In meeting minimal federal specifications, noninsulated security containers must satisfactorily pass a drop test of:

A.
15 feet

B.
20 feet

C.
22 feet

D.
25 feet

E.
30 feet

Answer: E
Explanation:

QUESTION NO: 291

In meeting minimal federal specifications, government security containers must be equipped with a combination lock capable of resisting manipulation and radiological attack for:

A.
10 man-hours

B.
20 man-hours

C.
30 man-hours

D.
40 man-hours

E.
45 man-hours

Answer: B
Explanation:

QUESTION NO: 292

Which of the following is not an approved UL safe classification?

A.
350-1

B.
350-2

C.
350-3

D.
350-4

E.
None of the above

Answer: C
Explanation:

QUESTION NO: 293

Underwriters Laboratories does independent testing on security containers that simulate a major fire where the heat builds up gradually to:

A.
7500P

B.
10000P

C.
20000P

D.
25000p

E.
30000P

Answer: C
Explanation:

QUESTION NO: 294

The acceptable vault construction of insulated doors has a minimum reinforced concrete wall, floor, and ceiling of:

A.
4 feet

B.
6 feet

C.
8 feet

D.

10 feet

E.
12 feet

Answer: B
Explanation:

QUESTION NO: 295

Which of the following would be a UL computer media storage classification?

A.
100-4

B.
150-4

C.
250-4

D.
350-4

E.
450-4

Answer: B
Explanation:

QUESTION NO: 296

Safes that are UL classified must be anchored to the floor or must weigh at least:

A.
750 lbs.

B.
1000 lbs.

C.

1500 lbs.

D.
2000 lbs

E.
3000 lbs.

Answer: A
Explanation:

QUESTION NO: 297

Which of the following is not generally true regarding money safes?

A.
Those manufactured prior to 1960 have round doors.

B.
They provide good protection against fire.

C.
They always have wheels.

D.
Today, money safes have square doors.

E.
Both B and C

F.
All of the above

Answer: E
Explanation:

QUESTION NO: 298

A "re-lock" on a vault door will automatically prevent the bolt mechanism from operating when:

A.

A timer is used.

B.
A switch is flipped.

C.
There is an attack on the door or the combination lock.

D.
It is locked by remote control.

E.
All of the above.

Answer: C
Explanation:

QUESTION NO: 299

Money safes are classified by both Underwriters Laboratories and:

A.
The Bureau of Standards

B.
The American Society for Industrial Security

C.
The Federal Deposit Insurance Corporation

D.
The Insurance Services Office

Answer: D
Explanation:

QUESTION NO: 300

Security vaults differ from safes in that:

A.

They do not have both fire- and burglary-resistant properties.

B.
Steel is used.

C.
They are tested by UL for burglary resistance.

D.
They are permanently affixed to the building.

E.
None of the above.

Answer: D
Explanation:

QUESTION NO: 301

Most theft is committed by:

A.
Professionals

B.
Organized crime

C.
Amateurs

D.
Maladjusted criminals

E.
Semiprofessionals

Answer: C
Explanation:

QUESTION NO: 302

An experienced safecracker will ordinarily use which of the following methods?

A.
Trying the maintenance standard combination

B.
Trying the day combination

C.
Trying the handle

D.
All of the above

E.
None of the above

Answer: D
Explanation:

QUESTION NO: 303

Which of the following methods has not been used in recent year to crack open record and money safes?

A.
Punching

B.
Core drilling

C.
Using a fluoroscope

D.
Torching

E.
Using a laser beam

Answer: E
Explanation:

QUESTION NO: 304

The weakness of the burning bar as a burglar tool is that:

A.
It will not burn through concrete.

B.
Its actual heat is not intense enough.

C.
It requires hydrogen tanks.

D.
It produces a large volume of smoke.

E.
All of the above.

Answer: D
Explanation:

QUESTION NO: 305

A 50 percent insurance discount is generally allowed to protect a safe if:

A.
The premises are guarded by security guards.

B.
The premises are open 24 hours a day.

C.
Multiple coverage is purchased.

D.
The safe is UL tested.

E.
The safe has wheels.

Answer: B
Explanation:

QUESTION NO: 306

Which of the following is not correct with regard to safes?

A.
Money safes do not have accredited fire resistance.

B.
UL classification labels are removed from all safes exposed to fires.

C.
Record safes are designed to resist fires only.

D.
Quality equipment should be purchased only from reputable dealers.

E.
Insulation in record safes more than 30 years old may negate fire-resistant qualities.

F.
None of the above.

Answer: F
Explanation:

QUESTION NO: 307

The UL symbol "TRTL" indicates:

A.
The type of locking devices used

B.
That the safe is resistant to both torches and tools

C.
That the safe is resistant to torches

D.
That the safe is resistant to tools

E.
None of the above

Answer: B
Explanation:

QUESTION NO: 308

Vaults are designed to meet most fire protection standards that are specified by the:

A.
Local fire department

B.
American Society for Industrial Security

C.
National Fire Protection Association

D.
All of the above

E.
None of the above

Answer: C
Explanation:

QUESTION NO: 309

Fire-resistant safes must pass which of the following tests?

A.
Explosion

B.
Impact

C.
Fire exposure

D.
All of the above

E.

None of the above

Answer: D
Explanation:

QUESTION NO: 310

Which of the following methods of attacking newer-model safes is considered to be impractical?

A.
Peel

B.
Punch

C.
Burn

D.
Manipulation

E.
Explosion

Answer: D
Explanation:

QUESTION NO: 311

The temperature that paper may be destroyed at is:

A.
200°F

B.
250°F

C.
300°F

D.

350°F

E.
400°F

Answer: D
Explanation:

QUESTION NO: 312

Electronic data and material can begin to deteriorate at:

A.
l00°F

B.
125°F

C.
150°F

D.
200°F

E.
300°F

Answer: C
Explanation:

QUESTION NO: 313

The maximum safe period of fire-resistant vaults is:

A.
Two hours

B.
Four hours

C.

Six hours

D.
Seven hours

E.
Eight hours

Answer: C
Explanation:

QUESTION NO: 314

The interior height of a vault should not exceed:

A.
8 feet

B.
9 feet

C.
10 feet

D.
11 feet

E.
12 feet

Answer: E
Explanation:

QUESTION NO: 315

The roof of a vault should be at least:

A.
3 inches thick

B.

4 inches thick

C.
5 inches thick

D.
6 inches thick

E.
8 inches thick

Answer: D
Explanation:

QUESTION NO: 316

The control of traffic through entrances and exits of a protected area is referred to as:

A.
Access control

B.
Patrol management

C.
Traffic stops

D.
Traffic management

E.
None of the above

Answer: A
Explanation:

QUESTION NO: 317

A system whereby the alarm signal is heard only in the immediate vicinity of the protected area is known as a:

A.
Local alarm system

B.
Proprietary system

C.
Central alarm system

D.
Portable alarm system

E.
None of the above

Answer: A
Explanation:

QUESTION NO: 318

A system using inaudible sound waves to detect the presence of an intruder or other disturbance is known as a(n):

A.
Motion detection system

B.
Ultrasonic motion detection system

C.
Sonic motion detection system

D.
Vibration detection system

E.
None of the above

Answer: B
Explanation:

QUESTION NO: 319

Which one of the following is true regarding structural barriers?

A.
Structural barriers serve as psychological deterrents.

B.
The objective of barriers is to cause as much delay as possible.

C.
A series of barriers are usually used in any effective physical protection plan.

D.
A series of concentric barriers should separate the area to be protected.

E.
Even with good planning, most structural barriers do not prevent penetration by humans.

F.
All of the above.

Answer: F
Explanation:

QUESTION NO: 320

Which of the following is not true regarding the use of security doors as barriers?

A.
Locking hardware is an important aspect of door security.

B.
The doorframe may be a weak point if not properly installed.

C.
Door hinges may add to the weakness of a door if not properly installed.

D.
The door is usually stronger than the surface into which it is set.

E.
All of the above.

Answer: D

Explanation:

QUESTION NO: 321

The weakest area in a window is usually:

A.
The frame

B.
The glass

C.
The sash

D.
Caulking

E.
Both A and D

F.
All of the above

Answer: C
Explanation:

QUESTION NO: 322

Which of the following is considered to be the most resistant to a blast explosion?

A.
Steel-frame building walls

B.
Thick brick or concrete walls

C.
Thick earthen barricades

D.
Thick reinforced concrete walls

E.
Wire-reinforced glass windows

Answer: D
Explanation:

QUESTION NO: 323

Two sheets of ordinary glass bonded to an intervening layer of plastic material that is used in street-level windows and displays that need extra security is known as:

A.
Tempered glass

B.
Plastic-coated glass

C.
Vinyl-coated glass

D.
Laminated glass

E.
Plate glass

Answer: D
Explanation:

QUESTION NO: 324

Bullet-resistant glass is made of:

A.
Reflected glass

B.
Plate glass

C.
Insulated glass

D.
Laminated glass

E.
None of the above

Answer: D
Explanation:

QUESTION NO: 325

What type of glass would be better for a storefront in terms of resistance to breakage, resistance to heat or extreme cold and resistance to overall deterioration?

A.
Laminated glass

B.
Wired glass

C.
Plate glass

D.
Acrylic material

E.
Bullet-resistant glass

Answer: E
Explanation:

QUESTION NO: 326

The type of glass that is often used for both safety and security purposes because it is three to five times stronger than regular glass and five times as resistant to heat is:

A.
Reflective glass

B.
Coated glass

C.
Wired glass

D.
Tempered glass

E.
None of the above

Answer: D
Explanation:

QUESTION NO: 327

The most widely used security device is:

A.
An alarm systems

B.
A lock-and-key device

C.
Protective lighting

D.
CCTV

E.
A fence

Answer: B
Explanation:

QUESTION NO: 328

Which of the following locks has been in use the longest and has no security value?

A.
The disc-tumbler lock

B.
The warded lock

C.
The wafer lock

D.
The pin-tumbler lock

E.
The lever lock

Answer: B
Explanation:

QUESTION NO: 329

The lock that is mostly used today for cabinets, lockers, and safe deposit boxes is:

A.
The wafer lock

B.
The disc-tumbler lock

C.
The pin-tumbler lock

D.
The lever lock

E.
Any locking device

Answer: D
Explanation:

QUESTION NO: 330

The most widely used lock in the United States today for exterior building doors and interior room doors is:

A.
The disc-tumbler lock

B.
The pin-tumbler lock

C.
The lever lock

D.
The wafer lock

E.
None of the above

Answer: B
Explanation:

QUESTION NO: 331

The best-known performance standard for guidance on the criteria of effective locking systems is published by:

A.
Medeco

B.
The Bureau of Standards

C.
Underwriters Laboratories

D.
Best Access Systems

E.
None of the above

Answer: C
Explanation:

QUESTION NO: 332

UL standards for the resistance to picking to align tumblers should be at least:

A.
3 minutes

B.
5 minutes

C.
10 minutes

D.
20 minutes

E.
30 minutes

Answer: C
Explanation:

QUESTION NO: 333

The sensor that is used when air turbulence is present in the room being protected and when there are no potential false alarm sources outside the room and in the field of the detector is a (n):

A.
Vibration detector

B.
Microwave motion detector

C.
Ultrasonic motion detector

D.
Acoustic detector

E.
None of the above

Answer: B
Explanation:

QUESTION NO: 334

The sensor that is used when light air turbulence, vibration, or motion is present outside the room is a(n):

A.
Vibration detector

B.
Microwave motion detector

C.
Ultrasonic motion detector

D.
Acoustic detector

E.
None of the above

Answer: D
Explanation:

QUESTION NO: 335

Foil used as a detector on a glass window to signal a surreptitious or forcible entry is an example of a(n):

A.
Vibration sensor

B.
Microwave sensor

C.
Capacitance sensor

D.

Acoustic sensor

E.
Electromechanical sensor

Answer: E
Explanation:

QUESTION NO: 336

The type of sensor that is designed to place a current-carrying conductor between an intruder and an area to be protected is known as a(n):

A.
Vibration sensor

B.
Microwave sensor

C.
Capacitance sensor

D.
Acoustic sensor

E.
Electromechanical sensor

Answer: E
Explanation:

QUESTION NO: 337

Which of the following does not pertain to the foil-type sensor?

A.
The cost of installation is cheap.

B.
The cost of the sensor is cheap.

C.
It acts as a psychological deterrent.

D.
It is subjected to false alarms because of breaks.

E.
Small cracks in the tape, or foil, will disable it.

F.
All of the above.

Answer: A
Explanation:

QUESTION NO: 338

The kind of sensor that is based on the Doppler principle, named after the Austrian scientist who originated the concept, is a(n):

A.
Capacitance sensor

B.
Electromechanical sensor

C.
Microwave sensor

D.
Acoustic sensor

E.
Photo sensor

Answer: C
Explanation:

QUESTION NO: 339

The sound wave sensor is commonly referred to as a(n):

A.
Radar detector

B.
Proximity detector

C.
Vibration detector

D.
Ultrasonic detector

E.
Electromechanical sensor

Answer: D
Explanation:

QUESTION NO: 340

The type of sensor that is not influenced by exterior noise, reacts only to movement within a protected area, and can also be adjusted to the movement of air caused by a fire to activate the alarm is known as a(n):

A.
Proximity sensor

B.
Radar sensor

C.
Vibration sensor

D.
Ultrasonic sensor

E.
Microwave sensor

Answer: D
Explanation:

QUESTION NO: 341

An alarm system that uses a sound- or light-generating device, such as a bell or strobe lights, located on the exterior wall of the protective area to call attention to a violation is known as a(n):

A.
Intruder alarm

B.
Local alarm

C.
Direct alarm

D.
Proprietary alarm

E.
Central station alarm

Answer: B
Explanation:

QUESTION NO: 342

An alarm system that is monitored by security personnel under the control of the owner of the establishment being protected is known as a(n):

A.
Intruder alarm

B.
Local alarm

C.
Direct alarm

D.
Proprietary alarm

E.
Central station alarm

Answer: D
Explanation:

QUESTION NO: 343

A specially constructed microphone attached directly to an object or surface to be protected and that responds only when the protected object or surfaced is disturbed is known as a:

A.
Special acoustic microphone

B.
Parabolic microphone

C.
Contact microphone

D.
Radio frequency microphone

E.
Vibration microphone

Answer: C
Explanation:

QUESTION NO: 344

A visual indicator that displays several zones or buildings in which an alarm signal has originated from is called a(n):

A.
Zone alarm panel

B.
Contact alarm panel

C.
Break alarm panel

D.
Annunciator

E.
Trouble signal

Answer: D
Explanation:

QUESTION NO: 345

Which of the following is true regarding CCTV?

A.
CCTVs reduce the amount of security personnel assigned to monitor entrances and exits.

B.
CCTVs are effective for control of personnel at entrances.

C.
CCTVs can be used as a psychological deterrent.

D.
CCTVs are equipped with pan/tilt/zoom and digital recording features.

E.
Both A and B.

F.
All of the above.

Answer: F
Explanation:

QUESTION NO: 346

The most critical component of all security processes is:

A.
Information

B.
Personnel

C.
Physical location

D.
Perimeter

E.
Intrusion control

Answer: B
Explanation:

QUESTION NO: 347

A comprehensive personnel security program should include:

A.
Adequate job specifications and performance standards

B.
Truth verification standards

C.
Appropriate selection and recruitment criteria

D.
Both A and B

E.
All of the above

F.
None of the above

Answer: E
Explanation:

QUESTION NO: 348

The standard of employment of military and government personnel was established by which executive order?

A.
11596

B.
12300

C.
9450

D.
1099

E.
1045

Answer: E
Explanation:

QUESTION NO: 349

The real meaning of the governmental policy in personnel security is:

A.
To hire only those who have high IQ test scores

B.
To keep those considered to be "risky" from obtaining jobs that are considered sensitive

C.
To detect and fire those found disloyal

D.
Both A and C

E.
All of the above

F.
None of the above

Answer: B
Explanation:

QUESTION NO: 350

When an individual is eligible to have access to classified information, this is called:

A.
A security clearance

B.
A Q clearance

C.
An FBI clearance

D.
A VIP clearance

E.
A field operative clearance

Answer: A
Explanation:

QUESTION NO: 351

Which of the following security clearances is not used by the government?

A.
Top secret

B.
Secret

C.
Confidential

D.
Restricted

E.

Q clearance

Answer: D
Explanation:

QUESTION NO: 352

What agency is responsible for processing requests for security clearances?

A.
The Federal Bureau of Investigation

B.
The Department of Justice

C.
The Central Intelligence Agency

D.
The National Security Council

E.
The Department of Defense

Answer: E
Explanation:

QUESTION NO: 353

Individuals who are not U.S. citizens, or are immigrants, are not eligible for security clearances except under reciprocal clearance involving:

A.
Israel and Canada

B.
NATO countries

C.
Canada and the United Kingdom

D.
Canada and NATO countries

E.
Both C and D

F.
None of the above

Answer: C
Explanation:

QUESTION NO: 354

Which is a type of personnel security investigation?

A.
National Agency Check

B.
Pre-employment

C.
Background investigation

D.
Department of Defense investigation

E.
Both A and C

F.
Both C and D

Answer: E
Explanation:

QUESTION NO: 355

An investigation that consists of checking the records of appropriate federal agencies for information bearing on the loyalty and suitability of a person under investigation is known as a(n):

A.
FBI investigation

B.
National Agency Check

C.
Loyalty investigation

D.
Background investigation

E.
Full field investigation

Answer: B
Explanation:

QUESTION NO: 356

A National Agency Check consists of:

A.
CIA records

B.
Civil Service records

C.
Coast Guard records

D.
Both A and B

E.
All of the above

Answer: E
Explanation:

QUESTION NO: 357

A background investigation for a security clearance consists of:

A.
Checking college attendance, if attended

B.
Verifying service in the armed forces

C.
Interviewing character references

D.
Both B and C

E.
All of the above

Answer: E
Explanation:

QUESTION NO: 358

During a security clearance background investigation, verification of naturalization will primarily be done by:

A.
Checking State Department records

B.
Checking FBI records

C.
Checking records of appropriate U.S. district courts

D.
Checking records of the Bureau of Vital Statistics

E.
All of the above

Answer: C
Explanation:

QUESTION NO: 359

The Act passed to require that consumer reporting agencies adopt reasonable procedures for meeting the needs of commerce for consumer credit is commonly known as:

A.
The Uniform Credit Act

B.
The Fair Credit Reporting Act

C.
The Consumer Relief Act

D.
The Consumer Reporting Act

E.
The Commercial Credit Act

Answer: B
Explanation:

QUESTION NO: 360

During a security clearance background investigation, when travel outside the United States is detected, which of the following should be checked?

A.
FBI records

B.
CIA records

C.
Immigration records

D.
Customs records

E.
All of the above

F.
None of the above

Answer: F
Explanation:

QUESTION NO: 361

The attitude or state of mind through which individuals are conscious of the existence of the security program and are persuaded that it is relevant to their own behavior is a concept known as:

A.
Security motivation

B.
Security awareness

C.
Security consciousness

D.
None of the above

Answer: B
Explanation:

QUESTION NO: 362

The theory that the human organism is motivated by an ascending series of needs and that once the lower needs have been satisfied they will be supplanted by the higher needs as motives for behavior is known as:

A.
Maslow's "Hierarchy of Prepotency"

B.
McGregor's Theory X

C.
McGregor's Theory Y

D.
Herzberg's Two Factor Theory

E.
Both B and C

F.
None of the above

Answer: A
Explanation:

QUESTION NO: 363

Security awareness is motivated by what technique?

A.
Integration into line operations

B.
Formal security briefings

C.
Use of written material

D.
Both B and C

E.
All of the above

F.
None of the above

Answer: A
Explanation:

QUESTION NO: 364

Which of the following is not an example of an intelligence test?

A.
Manual placement test

B.
Stanford-Binet IQ test

C.
Armed Forces General Classification Test

D.
Henman-Nelson IQ test

E.
None of the above

Answer: A
Explanation:

QUESTION NO: 365

An example of an honesty test given by firms to determine dishonest employees is:

A.
The Stanford-Binet test

B.
The Reid survey

C.
The Minnesota Multiphase Personality Inventory (MMPI)

D.
Both B and C

E.
All of the above

Answer: B
Explanation:

QUESTION NO: 366

A personality test that uses the MMPI evaluation and states it is specially designed for police and security applicants is:

A.
The Caldwell report

B.
The Reid survey

C.
The Stanford-Binet test

D.
The Stanton survey

E.
None of the above

Answer: A
Explanation:

QUESTION NO: 367

The main hurdle to overcome for personality tests is the requirement of the Civil Rights Act of 1964 that such a test not be discriminatory against protected minorities. This rule used as a test is known as the:

A.
30 percent rule

B.
40 percent rule

C.
60 percent rule

D.
80 percent rule

E.
None of the above

Answer: D
Explanation:

QUESTION NO: 368

According to a 1979 survey by the American Society for Industrial Security, the number of organizations in the United States offering security courses is greater than:

A.
50

B.
75

C.
150

D.
180

E.
250

Answer: D
Explanation:

QUESTION NO: 369

What are the advantages of having an outside organization perform background screening on your employees?

A.
Company personnel are spared potential embarrassments as well as liability claims.

B.
Depending on the number of checks, the costs will be lower.

C.
Screening will be done by trained staff with extensive sources of information.

D.

Screenings will be unbiased with no corrupt motivation.

E.
All of the above.

Answer: E
Explanation:

QUESTION NO: 370

Background investigations of an applicant should:

A.
Be based on the application and an interview record form

B.
Be done by a carefully screened investigator

C.
Be conducted without any prior contact from the applicant by the investigator

D.
All of the above

E.
None of the above

Answer: D
Explanation:

QUESTION NO: 371

Which of the following is not a requirement for handling preemployment interviews?

A.
Interviews must be voluntary.

B.
Interviews must be unbiased.

C.

For an interview to be effective, it should be conducted with a witness or a friend of the applicant present.

D.
The interviewer should not give out information.

E.
Complete and accurate notes should be taken.

Answer: C
Explanation:

QUESTION NO: 372

The quality of service rendered by security personnel is determined by which of the following?

A.
Personnel selection process

B.
Training

C.
Wages

D.
Supervision

E.
All of the above

Answer: E
Explanation:

QUESTION NO: 373

A Burns Security Survey covering 847 banks found that the most important single step toward improved crime prevention was:

A.

Adding more guards or public police

B.
Training bank employees

C.
Better security equipment

D.
Both B and C

E.
None of the above

Answer: B
Explanation:

QUESTION NO: 374

The basic principle of personnel security is:

A.
That education is the key to loss prevention

B.
That attitudes and honesty of rank and file employees are key to minimizing losses through theft

C.
To weed out bad apples among employees after they are located

D.
Both A and C

E.
All of the above

Answer: B
Explanation:

QUESTION NO: 375

Of the following questions, what cannot be asked of an applicant because of federal laws?

A.
Whether an applicant is married, divorced, separated, widowed, or single

B.
Whether an applicant owns or rents a residence

C.
Whether an applicant has ever been arrested

D.
Whether an applicant's wages have ever been garnished

E.
All of the above, except a

F.
All of the above

Answer: F
Explanation:

QUESTION NO: 376

Inquiring about an applicant's age and date of birth on a preemployment form may be prohibited by:

A.
The Civil Service Act of 1970

B.
Title VII of the Civil Rights Act of 1964

C.
The Age Discrimination in Employment Act

D.
All of the above

Answer: C
Explanation:

QUESTION NO: 377

Which of the following may be a clue on the employment form for considering refusal to hire?

A.
Gaps in employment history

B.
Long list of jobs over a relatively short period

C.
A significant reduction in salary at recent job

D.
Three to six months spent in the military

E.
All of the above

Answer: E
Explanation:

QUESTION NO: 378

Which of the following should not be a policy in considering applicants for hire?

A.
Similar problems in numerous areas, such as bad credit, absenteeism, numerous short-term jobs

B.
A problem in one area of interest should be enough to disqualify an applicant for hire

C.
If obviously overqualified, find out why applicant is willing to accept current job

D.
Both A and C

E.
All of the above

Answer: B

Explanation:

QUESTION NO: 379

Dishonest employees cost employers as much as all the nations' burglaries, car thefts, and bank holdups combined.

A.
A quarter

B.
Half

C.
The same amount

D.
Twice

E.
Triple

Answer: D
Explanation:

QUESTION NO: 380

According to estimates, about one third of all business failures are caused by:

A.
Theft from employees

B.
Bad management

C.
Theft from outsiders

D.
Poor quality of product or service

E.

None of the above

Answer: A
Explanation:

QUESTION NO: 381

Store inventory shortages are mainly caused by:

A.
Shoplifting losses

B.
Employee theft

C.
Poor inventory control

D.
Paperwork errors

E.
a, b, and d

F.
All of the above

Answer: E
Explanation:

QUESTION NO: 382

The single most important safeguard for preventing internal theft is probably:

A.
The personal interview

B.
Interviewing an applicant's references

C.

Use of the polygraph

D.
An extensive personal history search

E.
Upgrading the screening of new employees

Answer: E
Explanation:

QUESTION NO: 383

An employer may reject an applicant on the basis of:

A.
Incomplete data on the personal history search

B.
Unexplained gaps in employment history

C.
Unsatisfactory interview

D.
An arrest for a crime against property

E.
A conviction for a crime against property

Answer: E
Explanation:

QUESTION NO: 384

An employer may not question an applicant about:

A.
An unsatisfactory interview

B.

Unexplained gaps in employment history

C.
An arrest for a crime against property

D.
A conviction for a crime against property

Answer: C
Explanation:

QUESTION NO: 385

A study by scientists at Yale University (1939) found that theft resulted from:

A.
Lack of religion and moral values

B.
Aggression, frustration, and need

C.
Aggression, frustration, and lack of moral values

D.
Aggression, low morale, and low anticipation of being caught

E.
Aggression, frustration, and low anticipation of being caught

Answer: E
Explanation:

QUESTION NO: 386

Scientists at Yale University (1939) concluded that frustration almost always results in some aggressive reaction, the most important point being:

A.
Open aggression against the supervisor

B.
Aggression against the person whom the employee feels is responsible

C.
Unrelieved aggression builds up until relief from inner pressures becomes imperative

D.
A substitute satisfaction, in which the employee "gets even" by stealing from the company

Answer: D
Explanation:

QUESTION NO: 387

The theft triangle consists of the following components:

A.
Motivation, skill, and opportunity

B.
Opportunity, desire, and skill

C.
Motivation, opportunity, and rationalization (desire)

D.
Rationalization, skill, and opportunity

E.
None of the above

Answer: C
Explanation:

QUESTION NO: 388

Of those acquitted or dismissed by the courts for theft, over _____ percent were rearrested within 30 months.

A.
50

B.
60

C.
70

D.
80

E.
90

Answer: D
Explanation:

QUESTION NO: 389

Individuals who find integrity tests offensive are:

A.
Usually found to have a violent criminal past

B.
Sensitive individuals who do not like to take tests

C.
Twice as likely to be involved in some type of drug abuse behavior

D.
Twice as likely to admit to criminal activity or drug abuse

E.
None of the above

Answer: D
Explanation:

QUESTION NO: 390

A psychopath can often pass a polygraph test with a clean record because of the following characteristic:

A.
Uncooperative attitude

B.
Unstable personality

C.
An inferiority complex

D.
An abnormal lack of fear

E.
Both B and C

F.
All of the above

Answer: D
Explanation:

QUESTION NO: 391

Many experts agree that the most important deterrent to internal theft is:

A.
The chance of being fired

B.
Fear of discovery

C.
Threat of prosecution

D.
Guilt

E.
Lawsuits

Answer: B

Explanation:

QUESTION NO: 392

An employee should be questioned:

A.
With the door open

B.
With co-workers present

C.
Behind a closed door

D.
Behind a closed and locked door

Answer: C
Explanation:

QUESTION NO: 393

Frustration and aggression may be caused by:

A.
Increasing debts

B.
Personal problems

C.
Lack of recognition by superiors

D.
Dishonest supervisors

E.
The supervisor's lack of consideration in dealing with his or her employees or by unrealistic company policies

F.

All of the above

Answer: E
Explanation:

QUESTION NO: 394

An impelling type of leadership tends to reduce employee dishonesty because:

A.
It improves morale.

B.
It increases discipline.

C.
It sets a good example.

D.
It reduces employee frustration

E.
All of the above

Answer: D
Explanation:

QUESTION NO: 395

Stores that rely on stapling packages shut with the register tape folded over the top of the bag do this:

A.
To keep the customer from adding more items to the bag

B.
To show that the customer paid for the package

C.
To help the loss prevention officer

D.
For the psychological effect

E.
On the assumption that employees will not help each other

F.
All of the above

Answer: E
Explanation:

QUESTION NO: 396

Which of the following should the manager or supervisor immediately approve by signature?

A.
All voids and ove rrings

B.
All overrings and underrings

C.
All underrings and no sales

D.
All voids and overrings over a certain amount

E.
All of the above

Answer: D
Explanation:

QUESTION NO: 397

Overrings should not be corrected by undercharging on other items because this:

A.
Upsets the customer

B.
Confuses inventory controls

C.
Eliminates interaction by a manager or supervisor

D.
Is probably the easiest method of theft by employees

E.
All of the above

F.
None of the above

Answer: D
Explanation:

QUESTION NO: 398

The most effective deterrent to shoplifting is:

A.
Covert CCTVs

B.
Highly trained and educated loss prevention officers

C.
Well-trained personnel

D.
Sensor devices at the doors

E.
None of the above

Answer: C
Explanation:

QUESTION NO: 399

Employee complaints often arise from:

A.
Poor management

B.
Dissatisfaction

C.
Management having operating problems

D.
Employees airing their grievances

E.
A form of substitution for expressing their fears and frustrations concerning their personal lives

F.
All of the above

Answer: E
Explanation:

QUESTION NO: 400

Directional counseling of upset employees:

A.
Means giving advice

B.
May dominate the role for the manager or supervisor

C.
May be the wrong advice

D.
May be disturbing to the personnel director

E.
Is not usually desirable

Answer: E
Explanation:

QUESTION NO: 401

Nondirectional counseling of upset employees:

A.
Does not directly advise, criticize, or try to help

B.
Does not carry the danger inherent in giving advice

C.
Involves primarily being a good listener

D.
Should not be used because it is not effective

E.
None of the above

Answer: C
Explanation:

QUESTION NO: 402

The first skill the manager or supervisor must learn is:

A.
How to supervise or manage

B.
How to give orders

C.
How to check up on procedures

D.
The ability to listen

E.
How to maintain authority

Answer: D

Explanation:

QUESTION NO: 403

In the United States, employee thefts are:

A.
Fewer than thefts by shoplifters

B.
Fewer than the nation's burglaries

C.
Fewer than the nation's car thefts

D.
Equal to the nation's burglaries

E.
Greater than the problem of crime in the streets

Answer: E
Explanation:

QUESTION NO: 404

One thousand shopping tests across the nation showed that in a ten-year period, cash register thefts had increased by what percentage?

A.
46

B.
56

C.
66

D.
76

E.

Answer: E
Explanation:

QUESTION NO: 405

Personnel security problems are caused by:

A.
Dishonesty

B.
Disloyalty

C.
Disinterest of employees

D.
Low morale

E.
Both A and B

F.
All of the above

Answer: F
Explanation:

QUESTION NO: 406

Employees for the most part are:

A.
Honest

B.
Dishonest

C.

Disinterested

D.
Disloyal

E.
Conscientious, honest individuals who have the company's best interests at heart

Answer: E
Explanation:

QUESTION NO: 407

Employees' attitudes are directly affected by:

A.
The supervisor's attitude and actions

B.
Lack of recognition

C.
Personal problems that originate within and outside the company

D.
Fellow employees

E.
None of the above

Answer: C
Explanation:

QUESTION NO: 408

A major concern of a company, above all else, should be:

A.
Internal theft

B.

External theft

C.
Policies and procedures

D.
Reduction of shrinkage

E.
The care and well-being of its employees

Answer: E
Explanation:

QUESTION NO: 409

Searches made during work hours as a result of a bomb threat call should be made by:

A.
The fire department

B.
The local police department

C.
The Department of Army personnel

D.
The Federal Bureau of Investigation

E.
Employees familiar with the work area where the bomb is reportedly located

Answer: E
Explanation:

QUESTION NO: 410

The usual reaction of a corporation victimized by the kidnapping of an employee or extortion involving threat to lives of employees has been:

A.
To meet the negotiated demands of the terrorists

B.
To absolutely refuse to negotiate

C.
To negotiate but refuse to put up money

D.
To refer the terrorist to the police

E.
None of the above

Answer: A
Explanation:

QUESTION NO: 411

A cooperative organization of industrial firms, business firms, and similar organizations within an industrial community that are united by a voluntary agreement to assist each other by providing materials, equipment, and personnel needed to ensure effective industrial disaster control during emergencies is called a(n):

A.
Emergency squad

B.
Mutual aid association

C.
Community emergency cooperative

D.
Disaster control squad

E.
None of the above

Answer: B
Explanation:

QUESTION NO: 412

Which of the following procedures should not be advocated as part of emergency planning?

A.
Emergency plan should be in writing

B.
Emergency plan should be revised as needed

C.
Distribution of plan must be made down to the lowest echelons

D.
Distribution should be limited to senior management

E.
Plan should be tested through practice

Answer: D
Explanation:

QUESTION NO: 413

The federal agency in charge of disaster planning is the:

A.
Federal Emergency Management Agency

B.
Office of Civil Defense

C.
Department of the Army

D.
Department of the Interior

E.
Government Accounting Office

Answer: A
Explanation:

QUESTION NO: 414

The greatest single destroyer of property is/are

A.
Bombs

B.
Sabotage

C.
Fire

D.
Earthquakes

E.
Floods

Answer: C
Explanation:

QUESTION NO: 415

Responsibility for shutdown of a plant as a result of a disaster should be assigned to:

A.
The security office

B.
The board of directors

C.
The plant engineering service

D.
The accounting office

E.
The plant manager

Answer: C

Explanation:

QUESTION NO: 416

In the event the media makes contact as a result of a crisis situation, they should:

A.
Be given "no comment"

B.
Be put in touch with the person designated in the emergency plan for orderly release of information

C.
Be put in contact with the president of the company

D.
Be put in contact with the plant manager

E.
Be told to get in touch with the police

Answer: C
Explanation:

QUESTION NO: 417

First-aid training in regard to emergency planning can be obtained at no cost from:

A.
The local police

B.
The American Red Cross

C.
The fire department

D.
The local hospital

E.
The local high school

Answer: B
Explanation:

QUESTION NO: 418

Which of the following does not fit into good emergency planning?

A.
An individual should be appointed as coordinator.

B.
The plan should be in writing.

C.
The plan should be simple.

D.
A new organization should be developed to handle emergency situations.

E.
Key departments within the plant should be represented.

Answer: D
Explanation:

QUESTION NO: 419

In an emergency, planning records placed in storage should be in the form of:

A.
Microfilm

B.
Microfiche

C.
Computer tapes

D.
Any of the above

E.
None of the above

Answer: D
Explanation:

QUESTION NO: 420

The amount of combustible materials in the building is called:

A.
Fire-loading

B.
The combustion quotient

C.
The fire hazard level

D.
All of the above

E.
None of the above

Answer: A
Explanation:

QUESTION NO: 421

Which of the following is not an element in the classic fire triangle?

A.
Oxygen

B.

Heat

C.
CO2

D.
Fuel

E.
None of the above

Answer: C
Explanation:

QUESTION NO: 422

Most deaths from fire are caused by:

A.
Visible fire

B.
Panic

C.
Smoke or heat

D.
Inexperienced firefighters

E.
Inadequate equipment

Answer: C
Explanation:

QUESTION NO: 423

A fire involving ordinary combustible materials such as wastepaper and rags would be classified as:

A.
Class A

B.
Class B

C.
Class C

D.
Class D

E.
Class E

Answer: A
Explanation:

QUESTION NO: 424

Fires involving certain combustible metals would be classified as:

A.
Class A

B.
Class B

C.
Class C

D.
Class D

E.
Class E

Answer: D
Explanation:

QUESTION NO: 425

Fires involving live electrical equipment such as transformers would be classified as:

A.
Class A

B.
Class B

C.
Class C

D.
Class D

E.
Class E

Answer: C
Explanation:

QUESTION NO: 426

Fires fueled by such substances as gasoline, oil, grease, etc. would be classified as:

A.
Class A

B.
Class B

C.
Class C

D.
Class D

E.
Class E

Answer: B
Explanation:

QUESTION NO: 427

Soda and acid water based extinguishers are effective on:

A.
Class A fires

B.
Class B fires

C.
Class C fires

D.
Class D fires

E.
Class E fires

Answer: A
Explanation:

QUESTION NO: 428

Dry powder as a fire extinguisher is used on:

A.
Class A fires

B.
Class B fires

C.
Class C fires

D.
Class D fires

E.
Class E fires

Answer: D

Explanation:

QUESTION NO: 429

A carbon tetrachloride extinguisher would not be used on the following type of fire?

A.
Fire involving gasoline

B.
Fire involving grease

C.
Fire in a live transformer

D.
Fire in closed spaces

E.
All of the above

Answer: D
Explanation:

QUESTION NO: 430

The most effective extinguishing device known for dealing with Class A and B fires is:

A.
CO2

B.
Soda and acid

C.
Dry powder

D.
Water fog

E.
None of the above

Answer: D
Explanation:

QUESTION NO: 431

The ionization fire detector warns of fire by responding to:

A.
Invisible products of combustion emitted by a fire at its earliest stages

B.
Infrared emissions from flames

C.
Light changes

D.
Smoke

E.
Heat

Answer: A
Explanation:

QUESTION NO: 432

The fire detector that responds to a predetermined temperature or to an increase in temperature is known as a(n):

A.
Ionization detector

B.
Photoelectric smoke detector

C.
Infrared flame detector

D.
Thermal detector

E.
None of the above

Answer: D
Explanation:

QUESTION NO: 433

The fire detector that responds to an interruption in the light source. is known as a(n):

A.
Ionization detector

B.
Photoelectric smoke detector

C.
Infrared flame detector

D.
Thermal detector

E.
None of the above

Answer: B
Explanation:

QUESTION NO: 434

After a bomb threat has been received, the bomb search should be conducted by:

A.
The police

B.
The military

C.
The FBI

D.
The Bureau of Alcohol, Tobacco, and Firearms (ATF)

E.
Employees familiar with threatened areas

Answer: E
Explanation:

QUESTION NO: 435

One of the two most important items of information to be learned at the time of the bomb threat is the expected time of the explosion; the other is:

A.
Gender of caller

B.
Location of bomb

C.
Voice peculiarities of caller

D.
Motive of caller

E.
None of the above

Answer: B
Explanation:

QUESTION NO: 436

After a bomb threat is made, if a suspicious object is found during search, it should be:

A.
Handled with great care

B.

Disarmed immediately

C.
Reported immediately to the designated authorities

D.
Placed in a bucket of water

E.
None of the above

Answer: C
Explanation:

QUESTION NO: 437

The decision whether to evacuate a building as a result of a bomb threat will be made by the:

A.
FBI

B.
Police

C.
Management

D.
Military

E.
Employees' union

Answer: C
Explanation:

QUESTION NO: 438

If a bomb threat is an obvious hoax, the following action should be taken:

A.

Do nothing.

B.
Report the call immediately to the local police for investigation.

C.
Wait at least two hours to find out if the threat is actually a hoax.

D.
Contact the telephone company and report the call.

E.
Notify the Secret Service.

Answer: B
Explanation:

QUESTION NO: 439

The removal of any suspected bomb should be by:

A.
A proprietary guard force

B.
Office employees

C.
Professional bomb-disposal personnel

D.
The patrol office of the police department

E.
None of the above

Answer: C
Explanation:

QUESTION NO: 440

Which of the following fire losses is excluded from the widely used standard policy form?

A.
Military action

B.
Invasion

C.
Insurrection

D.
Civil war

E.
All of the above

Answer: E
Explanation:

QUESTION NO: 441

In order for an insurance policy to cover a burglary, there must be:

A.
Evidence of forcible entry

B.
A police report

C.
A police investigation

D.
Photos of the stolen property

E.
All of the above

Answer: D
Explanation:

QUESTION NO: 442

Which of the following is a requirement regarding kidnapping insurance?

A.
A kidnapping demand must occur during the policy period.

B.
Kidnap ransom is specifically made against the named insured.

C.
No disclosure of insurance is made outside corporate headquarters.

D.
All of the above.

E.
None of the above.

Answer: B
Explanation:

QUESTION NO: 443

Which of the following is not suggested behavior for the victim of a kidnapping?

A.
Stay calm.

B.
Do not cooperate with captors.

C.
Do not try to escape unless there is a good chance of success.

D.
Try to remember events.

E.
Do not discuss possible rescues.

Answer: A
Explanation:

QUESTION NO: 444

In setting up a plan to cope with kidnapping, the first contact should be with:

A.
Law enforcement

B.
The organization's executive committee

C.
Banking authorities

D.
The Federal Emergency Management Agency

E.
None of the above

Answer: A
Explanation:

QUESTION NO: 445

In connection with corporate kidnapping by terrorists, the decision as to whether ransom is to be paid should be made by:

A.
Local police

B.
The spouse or blood relative of the victim

C.
The FBI

D.
An employee at the highest corporate level

E.
None of the above

Answer: D
Explanation:

QUESTION NO: 446

A specific objective of the political kidnapper is:

A.
Publicity for cause

B.
Cash

C.
Penetration of a bank or other facility

D.
All of the above

E.
None of the above

Answer: D
Explanation:

QUESTION NO: 447

Responsibility for emergency "shutdown" should be assigned by the disaster plan to:

A.
The plant manager

B.
The plant security chief

C.
The plant engineering service

D.
The chairman of the board

E.
None of the above

Answer: C

Explanation:

QUESTION NO: 448

Which of the following should be part of a disaster recovery plan?

A.
Make one person responsible for health and sanitary conditions.

B.
Provide plan for emergency headquarters.

C.
Provide briefing for employees returning to work.

D.
All of the above.

E.
None of the above.

Answer: D
Explanation:

QUESTION NO: 449

The advantage of a mutual aid association in disaster planning is that it:

A.
Establishes a workable disaster control organization to minimize damage

B.
Helps ensure continued operation of the damaged facility

C.
Helps in restoring a damaged facility

D.
All of the above

E.
None of the above

Answer: D
Explanation:

QUESTION NO: 450

Which of the following should not be applicable to the development of an effective emergency disaster plan?

A.
The plan should be written.

B.
It should involve the minimum number of people possible in the preparation of the plan.

C.
It should contain an inventory of available resources.

D.
It should list preventative measures.

E.
None of the above.

Answer: B
Explanation:

QUESTION NO: 451

Once published, an emergency plan for disaster control should be distributed:

A.
On a need-to-know basis

B.
Only to the highest echelon

C.
Only to division heads

D.
Down to the lowest echelons assigned responsibility

E.
To none of the above

Answer: D
Explanation:

QUESTION NO: 452

The executive responsible for the development of the written emergency plan of an organization should be one who possesses which of the following qualifications:

A.
Technical aptitude

B.
Employment as a member of middle or senior management

C.
Complete familiarity with the company's organization

D.
All of the above

E.
None of the above

Answer: D
Explanation:

QUESTION NO: 453

A study in 1976 by the Institute for Disaster Preparedness at the University of Southern California revealed that the actual behavior of people during a post-disaster period was:

A.
Widespread panic

B.
Calmness

C.

Docile and "zombie-like"

D.
Antisocial

E.
All of the above

Answer: B
Explanation:

QUESTION NO: 454

Voluntary participation in disaster control activities may be motivated by:

A.
An interesting training program

B.
Training in fire fighting

C.
Training in bomb threat searches and related matters

D.
Instruction in safety and fire hazard control

E.
All of the above

Answer: E
Explanation:

QUESTION NO: 455

The correct procedure with respect to a bomb threat is that:

A.
Searches should be performed only when the call appears to be valid.

B.

Searches should always be conducted by the police.

C.
Personnel in work areas should not participate in searches.

D.
All of the above.

E.
None of the above.

Answer: E
Explanation:

QUESTION NO: 456

In emergency plans concerning a bomb threat, such a plan should require:

A.
Training for employees involved in searches

B.
A listing of telephone numbers of explosive disposal teams

C.
That, in evacuation, employees should ordinarily use exits other than main entrances

D.
All of the above

E.
None of the above

Answer: D
Explanation:

QUESTION NO: 457

Earthquake emergency plans should stress that the safest place. during a quake is:

A.

Within a work area under pre-selected cover

B.
In open spaces away from a building

C.
At home

D.
In a building made of concrete

E.
None of the above

Answer: A
Explanation:

QUESTION NO: 458

In a strike, the refusal by management to allow members of the bargaining unit on the premises is called a:

A.
Lockout

B.
Shutout

C.
Lock in

D.
All of the above

E.
None of the above

Answer: A
Explanation:

QUESTION NO: 459

The most important single relationship by a security organization with outside agencies during a strike is with:

A.
The fire department

B.
The hospital

C.
The police

D.
A prosecuting attorney

E.
None of the above

Answer: E
Explanation:

QUESTION NO: 460

At the time of a strike, if no guard force is available, the following action should be taken as a general rule:

A.
Immediately hire one.

B.
Mobilize supervisory personnel into a patrol group.

C.
Have police come on the property to act as a security force.

D.
All of the above.

E.
None of the above.

Answer: B
Explanation:

QUESTION NO: 461

During a strike the professional position of the police should be:

A.
To prevent violence

B.
To enforce laws firmly and fairly

C.
To suppress criminal conduct whenever it occurs

D.
All of the above

E.
None of the above

Answer: D
Explanation:

QUESTION NO: 462

Which of the following officers or employees will always be placed on a staff to develop an emergency evaluation and disaster plan?

A.
The finance office

B.
The personnel office

C.
The medical office

D.
The facility's security director

E.
The corporation's president

Answer: D
Explanation:

QUESTION NO: 463

Which of the following should not generally be incorporated in a company's emergency evacuation and disaster plan?

A.
Shutdown procedures

B.
Evacuation procedures

C.
Communications procedures

D.
Public information procedures

E.
A specific plan to deal with civil disturbances if conditions dictate

Answer: E
Explanation:

QUESTION NO: 464

The emergency evacuation and disaster plan should be:

A.
Detailed

B.
Tested initially

C.
Updated as required

D.
All of the above

E.
None of the above

Answer: D
Explanation:

QUESTION NO: 465

The activation of the company's emergency plan generally will be done by the:

A.
Security officer

B.
Plant manager

C.
Chairman of the board

D.
President of the company

E.
Personnel manager

Answer: B
Explanation:

QUESTION NO: 466

The National Bomb Data Center is operated by the:

A.
CIA

B.
FBI

C.
ATF

D.
LEAA

E.
Census Bureau

Answer: B
Explanation:

QUESTION NO: 467

The purpose of formulating a civil disorder plan is to:

A.
Ensure the safety and well-being of all personnel

B.
Ensure full protection of company property

C.
Ensure the continued operation of the facility

D.
Help bring about a peaceful solution of the community problem

E.
All of the above

Answer: E
Explanation:

QUESTION NO: 468

The civil disorder plan should be:

A.
Disseminated widely

B.
Restricted only to those responsible for formulating policy in connection with the plan and implementing it

C.
Posted on appropriate bulletin boards

D.
Disseminated only to security personnel

E.
None of the above

Answer: B
Explanation:

QUESTION NO: 469

A civil disorder planning committee should be staffed by which of the following?

A.
Director of security

B.
Personnel manager

C.
Facility manager

D.
All of the above

E.
None of the above

Answer: D
Explanation:

QUESTION NO: 470

With regard to civil disorder planning, the responsibility for maintaining law and order rests with:

A.
The FBI

B.
The Army Department

C.
Local authorities

D.
The proprietary security authority

E.
None of the above

Answer: E
Explanation:

QUESTION NO: 471

In connection with monitoring labor disputes, which of the following measures is not advisable?

A.
Change all perimeter-gate padlocks

B.
Issue special passes to no striking employees

C.
Notify employees who go to work to keep windows rolled up

D.
Provide armed guards

E.
All of the above

Answer: D
Explanation:

QUESTION NO: 472

Additional security personnel required to augment the regular security force during an emergency is usually accomplished by:

A.
Using the National Guard

B.
Using U.S. Army personnel

C.
Using uniformed guards from a private security company

D.
Using the facility's supervisory force

E.
None of the above

Answer: E
Explanation:

QUESTION NO: 473

Which of the following is generally used by saboteurs to disrupt industrial operations?

A.
Chemical means

B.
Electronic methods

C.
Fire

D.
All of the above

E.
None of the above

Answer: D
Explanation:

QUESTION NO: 474

Sabotage can effectively be combated by:

A.
Reducing target accessibility and vulnerability

B.
An effective training program

C.
A close liaison with FBI and other agencies

D.
All of the above

E.
None of the above

Answer: A
Explanation:

QUESTION NO: 475

The least often used method of sabotage is:

A.
Mechanical

B.
Fire

C.
Explosive

D.
Electronic

E.
Psychological

Answer: E
Explanation:

QUESTION NO: 476

In any strike procedure plan, all security personnel should be briefed by company management regarding:

A.
Company policy regarding the strike

B.
Property lines

C.
The importance of taking detailed notes of illegal activities

D.
All of the above

E.
None of the above

Answer: D
Explanation:

QUESTION NO: 477

Usually the most difficult part of an executive protection plan is:

A.
To secure trained personnel

B.
To initiate liaison with federal agencies

C.
To initiate liaison with local authorities

D.
To convince the executive being protected of the need for such protection

E.
None of the above

Answer: D

Explanation:

QUESTION NO: 478

Which of the following precautionary actions to provide executive protection is not advisable?

A.
Maintain a low profile.

B.
Do not use commercial airlines.

C.
Do not publicly announce travel.

D.
Consider use of armor-plated autos.

E.
None of the above.

Answer: B
Explanation:

QUESTION NO: 479

In a government-sponsored study of civil defense problems, the National Academy of Sciences and the National Research Council' predict that the strategic warning before a general nuclear war would be:

A.
Days to months

B.
Hours

C.
Minutes

D.
None

E.
Approximately 30 days

Answer: A
Explanation:

QUESTION NO: 480

Defense Readiness Condition (DEFCON) ratings - a numerical indication of world tension - are established by the:

A.
FBI

B.
NSA

C.
CIA

D.
NORAD

E.
State

Answer: D
Explanation:

QUESTION NO: 481

In emergency planning, vital records should be maintained at:

A.
The Emergency Operating Center (EOC) Record Center

B.
The National Archives in Washington, D.C.

C.
The company headquarters

D.
The local police department

E.
The Federal Emergency Management Agency

Answer: A
Explanation:

QUESTION NO: 482

Which of the following is a characteristic of a mail bomb?

A.
It was mailed from a foreign country.

B.
It is addressed to an individual by name or title.

C.
Its bulk and weight is greater than a normal airmail letter.

D.
All of the above.

E.
None of the above.

Answer: D
Explanation:

QUESTION NO: 483

Which of the following is an abnormal reaction to stress?

A.
Individual panic

B.
Depression

C.
Overactivity

D.
Bodily disability

E.
All of the above

Answer: E
Explanation:

QUESTION NO: 484

A type of bodily disability wherein a person unconsciously converts his or her anxiety into a strong belief that some part of his or her body has ceased to function is:

A.
Malingering

B.
Hysterics

C.
Conversion hysteria

D.
Depression

E.
Phobia

Answer: E
Explanation:

QUESTION NO: 485

Which of the following is not recommended as a preventive measure to prevent panic?

A.

Give people a routine to keep down anxieties.

B.
Don't emphasize discipline.

C.
Provide full and appropriate information to combat ignorance.

D.
Control rumors.

E.
None of the above.

Answer: B
Explanation:

QUESTION NO: 486

Which of the following is not a recommended action in planning for continuity of management during an emergency?

A.
Avoid assigning as alternatives for the same key positions people who reside in the same neighborhood.

B.
Keep top management from traveling together in the same vehicle.

C.
Tell only top executives of plan.

D.
Require at least yearly medical exams for key people.

E.
Prepare a job classifications file showing interrelated skills.

Answer: E
Explanation:

QUESTION NO: 487

Which of the following methods of duplication of records for emergency planning purposes is the least desirable?

A.
Handwritten notations

B.
Carbon copies

C.
Photocopying

D.
Microfilming

E.
None of the above

Answer: B
Explanation:

QUESTION NO: 488

The storage of records in vaults, safes, or storerooms on the premises rather than in dispersed storage is called:

A.
Dispersion

B.
Vaulting

C.
Restricted storage

D.
Physical protection

E.
None of the above

Answer: B

Explanation:

QUESTION NO: 489

Which of the following steps should be taken to provide viable emergency financial procedures?

A.
Provide for duplicate billing daily and proper record storage.

B.
Arrange vital files in readily portable units.

C.
Avoid hazardous areas for record storage.

D.
Have an adequate supply of actual cash on hand.

E.
All of the above.

Answer: E
Explanation:

QUESTION NO: 490

With regard to a nuclear attack, studies have shown that the numbers who would survive the initial effects of blast and heat would be:

A.
Tens of millions

B.
Less than 5 percent

C.
Less than 10 percent

D.
Less than 3 percent

E.

None of the above

Answer: A
Explanation:

QUESTION NO: 491

With regard to nuclear attack, depending on one's location and other circumstances, the following action should be considered for survival:

A.
Seek private shelter at home.

B.
Seek public shelter in your own community.

C.
Leave your community for shelter in a less dangerous area.

D.
All of the above.

E.
None of the above.

Answer: D
Explanation:

QUESTION NO: 492

A unit for measuring the amount of radiation exposure is called a(n):

A.
Gamma ray

B.
Roentgen

C.
Isotope

D.
Gamma meter

Answer: B
Explanation:

QUESTION NO: 493

With regard to a possible nuclear attack, the attack warning signal is a:

A.
30-second-long alarm

B.
2-minute-long alarm

C.
3-to-5-minute wavering sound on siren or a series of short blasts or whistle, etc.

D.
30-second wavering sound

E.
None of the above

Answer: C
Explanation:

QUESTION NO: 494

With regard to a potential nuclear attack, the attention or alert signal is usually a:

A.
30-second wavering sound on sirens

B.
30-second steady blast

C.
2-minute wavering sound

D.
4-minute wavering sound

E.
3-to-5-minute steady blast on siren

Answer: E
Explanation:

QUESTION NO: 495

Which action should not be taken if one hears a standard warning signal of potential nuclear attack?

A.
Go to a public fallout shelter.

B.
Go to a home fallout shelter.

C.
Turn on the radio.

D.
Telephone the nearest civil defense office for more information.

E.
None of the above.

Answer: D
Explanation:

QUESTION NO: 496

Which of the following is not a recommended treatment for a person who may be in shock?

A.
Keep the person lying down.

B.
Keep the person from chilling.

C.
Keep the person's head a little lower than his or her hips.

D.
Encourage the person to drink.

E.
Give the person alcohol to drink.

Answer: E
Explanation:

QUESTION NO: 497

A symptom of radiation sickness is:

A.
Lack of appetite

B.
Nausea

C.
Vomiting

D.
Fatigue

E.
All of the above

Answer: E
Explanation:

QUESTION NO: 498

Flood forecasts and warnings are issued by the:

A.
Federal Emergency Management Agency

B.
National Weather Service

C.
Department of the Interior

D.
National Oceanic and Atmospheric Administration

E.
Agriculture Department

Answer: D
Explanation:

QUESTION NO: 499

Which of the following is not a recommended action with regard to survival of earthquakes?

A.
If outside, immediately go inside.

B.
Keep calm.

C.
Douse all fires.

D.
Keep away from utility wires.

E.
Don't run through buildings.

Answer: D
Explanation:

QUESTION NO: 500

The firing train of a bomb generally consists of a:

A.
Detonator

B.
Booster

C.
Main charge

D.
All of the above

E.
None of the above

Answer: D
Explanation:

QUESTION NO: 501

Of all reported bomb threats, it is estimated that the percentage of real threats is:

A.
2 percent

B.
10 percent

C.
15 percent

D.
20 percent

E.
22 percent

Answer: A
Explanation:

QUESTION NO: 502

A full evacuation of a building should be ordered upon receipt of a bomb threat when:

A.
There is a reasonable suspicion that a bomb is present.

B.
Any threat is received.

C.
The threat is received during working hours.

D.
The caller has a foreign accent.

E.
None of the above.

Answer: A
Explanation:

QUESTION NO: 503

Which of the following may be an indication of a planted bomb?

A.
Loose electrical fittings

B.
Tin foil

C.
Fresh plaster or cement

D.
All of the above

E.
None of the above

Answer: D
Explanation:

QUESTION NO: 504

If a kidnapper warns the family of the victim not to notify police, the best course of action is to:

A.
Do nothing

B.
Contact a reliable detective agency.

C.
Notify the police anyway.

D.
Notify the telephone company.

E.
None of the above.

Answer: C
Explanation:

QUESTION NO: 505

The ZYX Corporation is in the process of relocating its facilities after several years of planning. The president, who is well aware of the necessity for emergency planning, directs you as the security manager to draw up necessary plans to cope with natural disasters. Which of the following is not a valid assumption to be considered?

A.
Some plants or facilities just are not vulnerable to natural disasters and therefore should not be involved in the planning.

B.
Most disasters considered likely will arrive with very little warning.

C.
Each plant and facility must be evaluated in terms of disaster, most likely to occur as well as the facility's capacity to cope with and minimize the effects of the disaster.

D.
In assessing the vulnerability of individual plants and other facilities, environmental, indigenous, and economic factors must be considered.

E.

Most disasters considered likely will have a rapid development and have a potential for substantial destruction.

Answer: A
Explanation:

QUESTION NO: 506

A natural hazard that poses a threat to many areas of this country is a hurricane. As soon as the weather forecaster determines a particular section of the coast will feel the full effects of a hurricane, he issues a hurricane warning. Such a warning specifies which of the following?

A.
Coastal areas where the eye of the storm will pass

B.
Coastal areas where winds of 74 mph or higher are expected

C.
Coastal areas where inhabitants should listen closely for further advisories and be ready to take precautionary actions

D.
The fact that there are definite indications a hurricane is forming and a name to the storm is given

E.
Coastal areas where winds are 100 mph or higher are expected

Answer: B
Explanation:

QUESTION NO: 507

One natural disaster that seems to occur with increasing frequency is the tornado. It is necessary for the security manager to be knowledgeable regarding all aspects of tornados so that adequate disaster plans can be formulated. Which of the following statements is incorrect?

A.
Tornados are violent local storms with whirling winds of tremendous speed that can reach 200-400 mph.

B.
The individual tornado appears as a rotating, funnel-shaped cloud that extends toward the ground from the base of a thundercloud.

C.
The tornado spins like a top, may sound like the roaring of an airplane or locomotive, and varies from gray to black in color.

D.
Tornados only occur in the middle plains, southeastern states, and some Middle Atlantic States.

E.
The width of a tornado path ranges generally from 200 yards to one mile.

Answer: D
Explanation:

QUESTION NO: 508

You are the security manager of the ZYW Corporation located in Phoenix, ArizonA.

A report is received from the national weather service that a tornado warning has been issued. Which of the following would be the correct action to take?

A.
Institute appropriate emergency notification procedures as this means that a tornado has actually been sighted in the area or is indicated by radar.

B.
Alert top management as this indicates tornados are expected to develop.

C.
Request the weather service to keep you advised on a 15minute basis.

D.
Have all windows in the facility closed and be alert to additional weather reports.

E.
Do nothing because tornados are usually not spotted in Arizona and the report is probably in error.

Answer: A
Explanation:

QUESTION NO: 509

As the security manager of a large corporation located in Southern California, you are charged with formulating a disaster plan to handle emergencies that arise as a result of earthquakes. Which of the following warnings to be issued to employees should not be included in the plan?

A.
If employees are outside, proceed to the nearest building and head for the basement promptly.

B.
If employees are indoors at the time of shaking, they should stay there.

C.
If inside, take cover under sturdy furniture.

D.
If inside, stay near the center of the building.

E.
If inside, stay away from glass windows and doors.

Answer: A
Explanation:

QUESTION NO: 510

Earthquakes constitute a definite concern to the emergency management responsibilities of security managers in certain areas of our country. Accordingly, it is incumbent upon security professionals to have a clear understanding of the basic facts concerning earthquakes. Which of the following is an incorrect statement?

A.
Earthquakes are unpredictable and strike without warning.

B.
Earthquakes may last from a few seconds to as long as five minutes.

C.
The actual movement of the ground in an earthquake is usually the direct cause of injury or death.

D.
Earthquakes may also trigger landslides and generate tidal waves.

E.
Most casualties during an earthquake result from falling material.

Answer: C
Explanation:

QUESTION NO: 511

Potential man-made disasters should be included when developing an emergency plan.

One of the most common man-made disasters is the plant fire. Which of the following is considered to be the most important aspect of plans for coping with major plant fires?

A.
To make certain that the plant's fire response team is adequately manned

B.
To make certain that the plant's firefighting equipment is adequate and in good operating condition

C.
To make certain plant personnel are well trained in firefighting techniques

D.
To make certain that there is a command center with excellent communications

E.
To make certain that mutual assistance agreements have been developed with local governments, other plants, and nearby installations

Answer: E
Explanation:

QUESTION NO: 512

Another area of potential concern from a disaster-planning standpoint is the handling, movement, and disposition of hazardous chemicals. Which of the following agencies is responsible for regulating the movement of hazardous chemicals?

A.
The Federal Bureau of Investigation

B.
The Interstate Commerce Commission

C.

The US. Department of Transportation

D.
The Department of Health and Human Resources

E.
The US. Department of Commerce

Answer: C
Explanation:

QUESTION NO: 513

Security managers must know all aspects of hazardous chemicals used in the plant, especially pertinent data concerning their locations, hazardous properties, characteristics, and potential hazardous reactions to each other. Which of the following is not a primary source of technical information on chemical hazards?

A.
The National Fire Protection Association, Boston, Massachusetts

B.
The Manufacturing Chemists Association, Washington, D.C.

C.
The National Agricultural Chemists Association, Washington, D.C.

D.
The Association of American Railroads

E.
The US. Department of Commerce

Answer: E
Explanation:

QUESTION NO: 514

Compared with other plant emergencies, bomb threats present a highly complex problem for plant management and emergency service personnel. Which of the following actions should not be in the bomb threat emergency plan as it is incorrect?

A.
Prior planning to meet the threat should include contact with a nearby military explosive ordnance disposal detachment (EODD).

B.
Prior planning should include contact with the local police department.

C.
Training programs for plant specialists in handling improvised explosive devices should be utilized when available from the military explosive ordnance disposal control center.

D.
The chief of police must make the decision whether or not to evacuate the building after a bomb threat has been received.

Answer: D
Explanation:

QUESTION NO: 515

One of the most difficult emergency decisions to be made involves the evacuation of a building because of a bomb threat, especially because statistics show that over 95 percent of such threats are hoaxes. Suppose your firm's switchboard operator receives such a threat, wherein the caller identifies himself as a member of a recognized terrorist group and gives the location of the bomb as to floor as well as the time of detonation. Which of the following actions should receive priority as to evacuation?

A.
Promptly consider evacuation.

B.
Call the FBI to have a subversive check made on the terrorist group.

C.
Secure advice from the FBI as to evacuation.

D.
Conduct a detailed search of the area involved and make a decision relative to evacuation after the search is completed.

E.
Do not evacuate, as odds are 95 percent in your favor that it is a hoax.

Answer: A

Explanation:

QUESTION NO: 516

An emergency plan with regard to bombs and bomb threats should include the steps to be taken if a bomb is located as a result of a search. Which of the following would be a proper procedure if the local police cannot dispose of an object that was located and thought to be a bomb?

A.
The FBI should be requested to dispose of the object.

B.
Volunteers in the plant should be utilized and instructed to handle the object carefully.

C.
The services of a bomb disposal unit should be requested.

D.
The U.S. Secret Service should be requested to handle the object.

E.
The object should be thoroughly isolated and defused by a robot.

Answer: C
Explanation:

QUESTION NO: 517

Complete and effective disaster planning should certainly include plans to deal with sabotage, as no plant is immune to sabotage. Which of the following is generally considered to be incorrect?

A.
Types of targets for sabotage as a rule cannot be predicted with any degree of accuracy.

B.
The saboteur will generally look for a target that is critical. vulnerable, and accessible.

C.
In general, saboteurs are enemy agents, disgruntled employee who commit sabotage for revenge, or individuals who are mentally unbalanced.

D.

The prevention of sabotage may be accomplished by reducing target accessibility.

E.
The methods of sabotage are varied and include psychological sabotage to cause slowdowns or work stoppage.

Answer: A
Explanation:

QUESTION NO: 518

The widespread and increasing industrial and commercial use and transportation of radioactive materials has increased the possibility, of radiological hazards resulting from accidents involving these materials. Which of the following is not a valid observation?

A.
If plant and local emergency services are not adequate to cope with the situation, federal assistance can be requested.

B.
Accidents may occur in facilities where radioactive material (are used or processed.

C.
In accordance with an interagency radiological assistance plan, the radiological emergency response capabilities of federal agencies can be used to protect public health and safety.

D.
Special emergency response capabilities have been established by the Environmental Protection Agency for coping with accidents involving nuclear weapons.

E.
When a radiological incident occurs in a plant, some degree of immediate response by state and local public safety personnel usually will be required.

Answer: D
Explanation:

QUESTION NO: 519

All security managers must have a disaster plan to deal with nuclear attack and must be well informed regarding the disaster propensities of such an explosion. The effects of nuclear weapons differ from those of conventional weapons in all of the following ways except:

A.
An experimental device exploded in the Aleutian Islands in November 1971 had an estimated yield of more than 5 megatons (MT), which means it released more energy than the explosion of 50 million tons of TNT.

B.
A fairly large amount of the energy in a nuclear explosion is referred to as "thermal radiation."

C.
"Thermal radiation" is capable of causing skin burns and of starting fires at considerable distances.

D.
A nuclear detonation also produces an electromagnetic pulse (EMP) sometimes called "radio flash."

E.
If a nuclear explosion occurs at or near the ground, great quantities of radioactive earth and other materials are drawn upward to high altitudes. When the radioactive particles fall back to earth, the phenomenon is known as "fallout."

Answer: A
Explanation:

QUESTION NO: 520

One of the greatest hazards that would result from a nuclear attack is radioactive fallout.

A security manager should be well informed concerning the full potential of damage associated with this type of disaster. Which of the following is an incorrect statement?

A.
Gamma radiation most concerns civil preparedness planners as it cannot be detected by any of the human senses.

B.
Gamma radiation is measured in units call roentgens.

C.
In an all-out nuclear attack against U.S. military, industrial, and population centers, it is estimated that severe to moderate damage from the blasts and heat effects would occur in about 50 percent of the nation's area.

D.

Gamma radiation can be detected only with special instruments.

E.
It is estimated that millions of Americans could survive the radiation effects of a large-scale nuclear attack by seeking protection in fallout shelters.

Answer: C
Explanation:

QUESTION NO: 521

The federal effort in preparing for a nuclear attack includes providing state and local governments with necessary advice and assistance. All of the following are valid observations regarding federal assistance except:

A.
The federal government has conducted a nationwide survey to identify fallout shelter space as part of the national shelter program.

B.
That, as a result of the national fallout shelter survey, it was determined that very few existing buildings contain usable shelter space.

C.
That nationwide radiological monitoring capability consists of several thousand federal, state, and local monitoring stations.

D.
That the National Warning System (NAWAS) has warning points strategically located throughout the continental United States.

E.
That the Emergency Broadcast System (EBS) is composed of nongovernmental radio and television stations.

Answer: B
Explanation:

QUESTION NO: 522

In emergency planning, nothing is more important than making sure that employees of your plant are thoroughly familiar with the National Attack Warning Signal. Which of the following is the correct signal?

A.
A la-minute wavering sound on siren

B.
A 3-to-5-minute steady sound on siren

C.
A series of one-minute steady sounds on sirens

D.
A 3-to-5-minute wavering sound on sirens or a series of short blasts on whistles, horns, or other devices as necessary

E.
A ringing of all church bells for 5 minutes

Answer: D
Explanation:

QUESTION NO: 523

At 1500 hours, you, as well as other employees of the ZYX firm, hear a 3-to-5-minute wavering sound on sirens. There has been no previous notification of an impending test of the siren system. If you have adequately done your job as security manager, the employees should recognize that the following action should be taken.

A.
Ignore it as there has been no confirmation that it is for real.

B.
Because this signal means an actual enemy attack against the United States has been detected, protective action should be taken immediately.

C.
Because this is merely an alert signal, proceed with normal activities until you are advised to take other action.

D.
Do nothing until the Federal Emergency Management Agency verifies the status of an emergency.

E.

Ignore it because most situations such as this have proven to be equipmentmal functions.

Answer: B
Explanation:

QUESTION NO: 524

The continuity of business and industrial leadership and direction are essential parts of all industrial emergency plans. The following specific measures should be included in the development of a plan for continuity of leadership except:

A.
Ensuring a functioning board of directors

B.
Establishing lines of succession for key officers and operating personnel

C.
Establishing an alternate company headquarters

D.
Providing for a special stockholder meeting immediately after attack to provide for methods of operation

E.
Ensuring record preservation

Answer: D
Explanation:

QUESTION NO: 525

In reviewing the emergency plans of the ZYX Corporation, the legal counsel of the firm notes that under nuclear disaster conditions there is a definite possibility that a quorum of the board of directors cannot be readily assembled, which will not allow action in accordance with law. Which of the following methods generally would not be acceptable to remedy this legal problem?

A.
Reduce the quorum number if allowed by state law.

B.
Fill board vacancies if allowed by state law.

C.
Establish an emergency management committee, if allowed by state law.

D.
Appoint alternate directors, if allowed by state law.

E.
Utilize a chain of command and execute proper power of attorney papers for the top three officials so the most senior could execute legal affairs if the board is not functioning.

Answer: E
Explanation:

QUESTION NO: 526

Provisions for the establishment of emergency lines of executive succession should be included in a company's emergency plans. Which of the following cannot be relied on as being valid in making decisions in this regard?

A.
The board of directors sets general policy.

B.
The board of directors is the entity legally responsible for corporate activity.

C.
The board of directors usually meets at stated times such as monthly or perhaps even only quarterly.

D.
Responsibility for day-to-day operations is vested in the officers.

E.
Generally speaking, state statutes usually vest specified functions in particular officers and usually set out in detail the duties of officers.

Answer: D
Explanation:

QUESTION NO: 527

As security manager of the ZYX Corporation, you have been instructed to devise company plans to protect vital records in the event of a disaster. You immediately realize the serious nature of such plans and begin to make appropriate plans.

Approximately what percentage of the company's records would normally constitute a company's vital records to be safeguarded during an emergency?

A.
2 percent

B.
5 percent

C.
8 percent

D.
10 percent

E.
20 percent

Answer: A
Explanation:

QUESTION NO: 528

In devising plans to protect vital records during an emergency. a prime decision to make would be the identification of vital records. Whether such records are vital depends to a large extent on the type of business conducted. However, as a general rule, all of the following would be considered vital to any corporate organization except:

A.
The incorporation certification

B.
Personal identification fingerprints of employees

C.
The by-laws of the corporation

D.
The stock record books

E.
Board of directors' minutes

Answer: B
Explanation:

QUESTION NO: 529

The selection of records to be protected under an emergency vital records protection program is a difficult operation. Which of the following statements is considered to be incorrect in making such a selection?

A.
Management should protect vital records by systematically determining what information is vital.

B.
The vital records protection program is an administrative device for preserving existing records.

C.
If a particular record does not contain vital information, it has no place in the company's vital records protection program even though it may have other value for the company.

D.
Decision making in determining individual vital records should be rapid. A record either contains vital information or it does not.

E.
Vital information is not necessarily on paper.

Answer: B
Explanation:

QUESTION NO: 530

Some of the vital company information that management seeks to protect is processed by a computer and captured on distinctive media associated with electronic data processing. Effective protection of this vital information is complicated for a number of reasons. Which of the following is incorrect in this regard?

A.
A nuclear detonation produces an electromagnetic pulse (EMP) that could cause considerable

damage. However, well-tested EMP-protective devices are available.

B.
Formerly dispersed information is consolidated, which intensifies its exposure to possible destruction or compromise.

C.
The data processing medium is extremely vulnerable to a wide variety of perils such as fire, water, dirt, and hazardous chemical gases.

D.
Both the computer and the area in which it is located must be protected along with the vital information.

E.
Information transmitted over a distance for remote computer processing is out of the company's direct control for an extended period of time.

Answer: A
Explanation:

QUESTION NO: 531

As the security manager of the ZYX Corporation, you have been given the responsibility of improving the security of the computer facility. Which of the following would least improve the security?

A.
Make the facility as inconspicuous as possible.

B.
Provide 24-hour security guard surveillance of the area.

C.
Strengthen controls over access to the facility.

D.
Make sure all unused wiring, including telephone cables, is neatly stored in the computer room.

E.
Wherever local fire codes permit, remove water sprinkler fire extinguisher systems and replace with carbon dioxide or halon 1301 systems.

Answer: D

Explanation:

QUESTION NO: 532

The vital records protection program is designed to protect and provide the information needed by the company for survival in a disaster or emergency. Periodic vital records protection program tests must be provided for to determine the adequacy of the protection program. Which of the following observations is incorrect?

A.
The company security officer, records manager, and internal auditor should test or evaluate the program at least once a year.

B.
Every effort should be made to make test conditions as realistic as feasible.

C.
Specifically, the test should determine that the company's various vital information needs can be satisfied in a typical emergency situation.

D.
The test period should not be limited in time but should be extended as long as needed.

E.
The test should be located off of company premises, if possible.

Answer: D
Explanation:

QUESTION NO: 533

The president of the ZYX Corporation expresses concern relative to the company's ability to act in an emergency to protect life and property. He instructs that you undertake the necessary action to establish the desired emergency capability within the facility. Which of the following should be the first step in initiating this action?

A.
Contact established guard companies to make bids to oversee the operations.

B.
Do nothing until funds have been appropriated.

C.
Appoint an emergency coordinator at the corporate level.

D.
Make a physical survey of the plant.

E.
Form a committee of key executives to operate out of the command level.

Answer: C
Explanation:

QUESTION NO: 534

Providing for proper succession of management in the event of a disaster is a key part of any disaster plan. Your prime responsibility in the development of a management successor list would be to select:

A.
Key personnel who have engineering degrees

B.
Those individuals who have been with the company in excess of 10 years

C.
Enough names so as to make sure that at least one person on the list would always be available during an emergency

D.
Those who hold an executive position of president, vice president, treasurer, or secretary

E.
Either the plant manager or security director to head the corporate emergency planning activities

Answer: C
Explanation:

QUESTION NO: 535

In establishing a disaster plan, provision should be incorporated that would permit you to be prepared for a variety of emergency situations. Which of the following probably would not have a key role in such plans?

A.
Employee welfare service

B.
Rescue teams

C.
The recreational coordinator

D.
The Radiological Defense Service

E.
The engineering service

Answer: C
Explanation:

QUESTION NO: 536

In any well-designed disaster plan, you as security manager have as a primary goal the achievement of "emergency readiness." Which of the following explanations most adequately defines the term "emergency readiness?"

A.
It means that you are prepared to react promptly to save life and protect property if your plant is threatened or hit by a major emergency or disaster of any type.

B.
It means that the Federal Emergency Management Agency has inspected and approved the company's disaster plans.

C.
It means that all security personnel have met minimum training standards of the state in which the plant is located.

D.
It means that all officials of the security department have successfully passed the Certified Protection Professional® CCPP) examination.

E.
It means that the security staff is 100 percent manned.

Answer: A

Explanation:

QUESTION NO: 537

Perhaps one of the most difficult tasks in planning for disaster and emergencies is the actual formulation of a basic disaster plan. Which of the following is an incorrect procedure in developing such a plan?

A.
The basic plan should provide for coordination of government and company actions before and during a disaster.

B.
A glossary of terms used should be included.

C.
There should be a listing of types of emergencies limited to those experienced by the company in the past.

D.
The plan should utilize appendices as needed, such as maps, call-up lists, and mutual aid agreements.

E.
The plan should specifically provide for coordination of government and company action before and during a disaster.

Answer: C
Explanation:

QUESTION NO: 538

Although protection of people is without a doubt the first priority in planning for emergencies, shutdown procedures must be thorough and done by those who are trained to do so. Your disaster plan should have such shutdown procedures assigned to:

A.
The security force

B.
The plant manager

C.
Maintenance employees on each shift who handle these procedures on a regular basis

D.
The fire brigade

E.
Supervisors of the plant

Answer: C
Explanation:

QUESTION NO: 539

Emergency shutdown procedures are of great importance because orderly shutdown measures may help avert damage and loss. Your emergency preparedness planning should provide for the following actions except:

A.
Such plans should be developed and tested by the department managers concerned.

B.
Time should not be wasted in attempting to move critical or valuable items inside.

C.
Personnel on each shift should be designated to close doors and windows.

D.
Section heads must complete shutdown check-off lists and supervise shutdown procedures in their particular areas.

E.
Precious metals and original drawings should be in locked storage or be moved to safer locations.

Answer: B
Explanation:

QUESTION NO: 540

After the disaster plan has been fully prepared and tested, you as the security manager must make certain that the employees thoroughly understand it and actually take an active interest in it. Which of the following should not be done in your program of informing and educating the employees as to the plan?

A.
Information disseminated to management should be prepared no differently from that contained in a general employee announcement.

B.
Safety committees playa very important role in the development of the emergency plan.

C.
Daily newsletters, bulletins, postings, and sales magazines should be closely evaluated as possible channels for the dissemination of disaster information.

D.
New employees should be made aware of the existence of the disaster plan as soon as they come on duty.

E.
Supervisory personnel are considered spokesmen for the company and employees naturally turn to these individuals for information.

Answer: A
Explanation:

QUESTION NO: 541

In order to adequately plan for emergencies, the security manager must make certain that the corporation has access to all necessary resources that will save lives, minimize damage, and ensure the continued operation of rapid restoration of damaged member plants. Most plants ensure access to such resources by:

A.
Providing for a budget that will supply all the resources needed to cope with a major emergency

B.
Establishing appropriate liaison with the police, fire, rescue, and medical forces of the community to provide services as needed

C.
Relying on their own self-help organization and equipment and joining hands with other plants in the community for mutual aid

D.
Establishing appropriate contact with the nearest military base

E.
Contracting with local security companies to provide necessary resources, if needed during an emergency

Answer: C
Explanation:

QUESTION NO: 542

In forming an industrial mutual aid association, a number of definitive plans must be made. Which of the following is not true and should not be relied on in formulating these plans?

A.
Each member firm must be willing to defray industrial mutual aid association expenses.

B.
Capital outlay and operating costs are usually modest.

C.
The basic operating element of a mutual aid association is an operating board.

D.
Any industrial mutual aid association should be established in advance of emergencies, not afterward.

E.
A small operating headquarters should be established where appropriate files and records can be maintained.

Answer: B
Explanation:

QUESTION NO: 543

A key role in any emergency will be played by the plant manager or, in his or her place, an authorized official such as the emergency coordinator or security chief. Which of the following should not be done personally by this official?

A.
Take personal charge of all operations at the disaster scene.

B.
Activate the plant control center.

C.
Alert and inform the local government emergency coordinator.

D.
Brief plant control center staff on the emergency situation.

E.
Mobilize employees and other resources to the extent required.

Answer: A
Explanation:

QUESTION NO: 544

No document associated with disaster planning is more important than the disaster plan manual. In preparing this manual, all of the following are applicable except:

A.
Do not clutter this manual with such minor items as the geographic location of the plant, site plans, floor plans, and utilities layouts.

B.
All plant emergency operations plans should be put in writing.

C.
Prepare and test the emergency plan before it is needed.

D.
Make the disaster plan manual distinctive by using a special color for the cover.

E.
Each plan should contain statements of company policy regarding emergency planning.

Answer: A
Explanation:

QUESTION NO: 545

The keys to the success of any emergency organization and plan are training and testing.

In designing effective testing procedures, the following are all valid observations except:

A.
Records should be maintained so deficiencies can be corrected following the test.

B.
The testing exercise should be as realistic as possible.

C.
Plenty of advance notice should be given so all possible preparations can be made.

D.
One of the best times to test the plant emergency plan is in coordination with your local government periodic test exercises.

E.
Testing of the emergency plan should require the actual operation or simulation of every element of the plan in all possible emergency conditions.

Answer: C
Explanation:

QUESTION NO: 546

What is considered an advantage of requiring minimum training requirements of security officers?

A.
Productivity increases dramatically with proper training.

B.
There is a sales and service advantage if trained guards are provided.

C.
It builds professionalism.

D.
Promotions are more easily made.

E.
Both A and C.

F.
All of the above.

Answer: F
Explanation:

QUESTION NO: 547

Which of the following procedures is recommended to motivate nighttime guards?

A.
Give the night shift an elite status.

B.
Pay for nighttime guards should be higher than for daytime guards.

C.
People should be "promoted" to being on the night shift.

D.
Make night jobs as attractive as possible.

E.
All of the above.

Answer: E
Explanation:

QUESTION NO: 548

Which of the following constitutes a prime responsibility entrusted to the guard force of a museum?

A.
Protection of objects of art against all hazards

B.
Enforcement of institution's rules and regulations

C.
The safety and well-being of visitors and the employees of the museum

D.
All of the above

E.
None of the above

Answer: D
Explanation:

QUESTION NO: 549

The Bank Protection Act specifies that each banking institution:

A.
Must have a security officer at each location

B.
Is not required to have a designated security officer

C.
Must have a security officer but not necessarily at each location

D.
Must have at least two security officers at each location

E.
None of the above

Answer: C
Explanation:

QUESTION NO: 550

Which of the following is considered to be an advantage of contracting for guard services?

A.
Lower payroll costs

B.
Fewer administrative headaches

C.
No absenteeism problems

D.
No collective bargaining

E.
All of the above

Answer: E
Explanation:

QUESTION NO: 551

Which of the following factors should be evaluated in considering the need for security officers to have weapons?

A.
The type of encounter to be faced by the security officer

B.
The nature of the potential threat

C.
The operational objective of the security officer

D.
All of the above

E.
None of the above

Answer: D
Explanation:

QUESTION NO: 552

Which of the following would be an argument against the use of nonlethal weapons by the security officer?

A.
They do not pose a substantial risk of death if used properly.

B.

They provide an alternative to guns where the situation requires less than lethal force.

C.
Use of nonlethal weapons reduces the risk of death to innocent bystanders.

D.
It might escalate confrontations with security officers because offenders would feel less threatened.

E.
None of the above.

Answer: D
Explanation:

QUESTION NO: 553

The issuance of weapons to guards is usually not justified:

A.
In a situation where deterrence is needed in handling a large amount of cash

B.
In situations in which terrorism is a real threat

C.
In a situation where there would be a greater danger to life without weapons than with them

D.
In a situation where there seems to be no danger to life without weapons

Answer: D
Explanation:

QUESTION NO: 554

In issuing policy statements regarding the handling of disturbed persons, the primary consideration is:

A.

Legal liability to the disturbed

B.
Reducing the disturbed person to a form of benevolent custody and eliminating the immediate danger

C.
Legal liability to employees and third persons if restraint is not achieved

D.
Employee-community public relations

E.
None of the above

Answer: B
Explanation:

QUESTION NO: 555

The argument usually used by contract guard representatives as a selling point in their services is:

A.
They are nonunion.

B.
There are no administrative problems.

C.
They are better trained.

D.
They provide a reduction in cost.

E.
Their objective is carrying out duties.

Answer: D
Explanation:

QUESTION NO: 556

The most important written instructions for the security guard are known as:

A.
Memoranda

B.
Operational orders

C.
Staff orders

D.
Post orders

Answer: D
Explanation:

QUESTION NO: 557

Which of the following should be a required criterion of the security guard's post orders?

A.
The order should be written at the lowest level possible.

B.
Each order should deal with multiple subjects.

C.
The order should be detailed.

D.
The order should be indexed sparingly.

E.
None of the above.

Answer: A
Explanation:

QUESTION NO: 558

The security guard's primary record of significant events affecting facility protection is known as the:

A.
Ingress log

B.
Egress log

C.
Security log

D.
Daily events recorder log

E.
Supervisor's log

Answer: C
Explanation:

QUESTION NO: 559

Estimates as to the number of security officers - both contract and proprietary - in the United States is approximately:

A.
250,000

B.
300,000

C.
500,000

D.
700,000

E.
1,000,000+

Answer: E
Explanation:

QUESTION NO: 560

A major study on private security was prepared by the:

A.
American Society for Industrial Security

B.
International Association of Chiefs of Police

C.
Private Security Task Force of the National Advisory Committee on Criminal Justice Standards and Goals

D.
Brookings Institute

E.
Harvard Symposium in Private Security

Answer: C
Explanation:

QUESTION NO: 561

The number of security guards required for a facility is determined by:

A.
Number of personnel

B.
Number of entrances and hours of operation

C.
Physical complexity of a facility

D.
Number of security guards required to protect the facilities

E.
Number of escorts or special assignments required

F.
All of the above

Answer: F
Explanation:

QUESTION NO: 562

What is the primary function of the security officer?

A.
Patrol of buildings and perimeters

B.
Inspection of security and fire exposures

C.
Access control

D.
Being a bodyguard

E.
Bomb threats

Answer: C
Explanation:

QUESTION NO: 563

Guard patrols are generally divided into what two categories?

A.
Specialized patrols and security patrols

B.
Nightwatch patrols and daywatch patrols

C.
Foot patrols and vehicle patrols

D.
None of the above

Answer: C
Explanation:

QUESTION NO: 564

Which of the following is not true of post orders?

A.
Most are important written instructions to the security force.

B.
They summarize the required security officers' duties.

C.
They express the policies of the facility being protected.

D.
They provide clear instructions.

E.
Most post orders include oral instructions to the security officer.

Answer: E
Explanation:

QUESTION NO: 565

Which of the following is not a true characterization of the guard operation?

A.
Security guards are costly.

B.
Security guards are generally recognized as an essential element in the protection of assets and personnel.

C.

Security guards are the only element of protection that can be depended on to give complete security.

D.
Security guards can also perform as public relations representatives when properly trained.

Answer: C
Explanation:

QUESTION NO: 566

Each guard post that is manned 24 hours a day, 7 days a week, requires:

A.
Two guards

B.
Three guards

C.
Four and a half guards

D.
Five guards

E.
Six guards

Answer: C
Explanation:

QUESTION NO: 567

The occupation of a uniformed security officer is psychologically:

A.
Extraordinarily high stress

B.
High stress

C.
Medium stress

D.
Low stress

E.
An easy occupation

Answer: B
Explanation:

QUESTION NO: 568

The basic or "organic" law of the United States is:

A.
Common law

B.
U.S. statutes at large

C.
U.S. Constitution

D.
Supreme Court decisions

E.
The Bill of Rights

Answer: C
Explanation:

QUESTION NO: 569

The only crime mentioned in the U.S. Constitution is:

A.
Treason

B.
Murder

C.
Extortion

D.
Fraud against the government

E.
None of the above

Answer: A
Explanation:

QUESTION NO: 570

In substance a crime is;

A.
A violent act

B.
A violation of one's property

C.
An act or omission prohibited by law that provides a punishment

D.
A public wrong

E.
A private wrong

Answer: C
Explanation:

QUESTION NO: 571

The federal criminal law is contained in:

A.
Title 1 of the U.S. Code

B.
Title 12 of the U.S. Code

C.
Title 18 of the U.S. Code

D.
Title 20 of the U.S. Code

E.
Title 48 of the U.S. Code

Answer: C
Explanation:

QUESTION NO: 572

The federal definition of a felony is:

A.
Any offense that calls for imprisonment

B.
Any offense punishable by death

C.
Any offense for which the minimum penalty is $500

D.
Any offense punishable by death or imprisonment for a term exceeding one year

Answer: D
Explanation:

QUESTION NO: 573

In general, an act will not be criminal unless the person engaged in the act has:

A.
Mens rea

B.
The necessary motive

C.
Knowledge of the criminal statute

D.
Actus rea

E.
None of the above

Answer: A
Explanation:

QUESTION NO: 574

Whoever has knowledge of the actual commission of a felony cognizable by a court of the United States but conceals and does not as soon as possible make known the same to some judge or other person in civil or military authority is guilty of the following violation:

A.
Subornation of perjury

B.
Obstruction of justice

C.
Misprision of felony

D.
White-collar crime

E.
None of the above

Answer: C
Explanation:

QUESTION NO: 575

In federal courts the usual prosecutor is known as:

A.
The district attorney

B.
The state's attorney

C.
The commonwealth attorney

D.
The U.S. attorney

E.
The special prosecutor

Answer: D
Explanation:

QUESTION NO: 576

The main purpose of a grand jury is to:

A.
Determine whether an individual has committed a crime or not

B.
Determine guilt

C.
Determine whether there is probable cause that a crime has been committed

D.
Determine the nature of punishment

E.
Give the accused the chance to face his or her accuser

Answer: C
Explanation:

QUESTION NO: 577

After an indictment has been returned by a grand jury, the person named must be taken into custody and appear personally before the appropriate court. This process is called a(n):

A.
Arraignment

B.
First appearance

C.
Preliminary hearing

D.
Magistrate's hearing

E.
Pretrial hearing

Answer: A
Explanation:

QUESTION NO: 578

The purpose of bail is to:

A.
Confine the accused pending trial

B.
Take dangerous offenders off the street

C.
Make certain each accused person is offered his or her constitutional right to put up security in order to gain release

D.
To ensure the appearance of the accused in court

E.
None of the above

Answer: D
Explanation:

QUESTION NO: 579

In a criminal trial the burden of proof required to find guilt is:

A.
Preponderance of evidence

B.
Beyond a reasonable doubt

C.
Reasonableness of presentation

D.
Amount necessary to convince a majority of jurors

E.
None of the above

Answer: B
Explanation:

QUESTION NO: 580

The release of a convicted person under certain conditions without having to be imprisoned is known as:

A.
Probation

B.
Parole

C.
Corpus juris

D.
Detainer

E.
Commutation

Answer: A
Explanation:

QUESTION NO: 581

The release from confinement of a person who has served part of a sentence is called:

A.
Probation

B.
Parole

C.
Reprieve

D.
Commutation

E.
Pardon

Answer: B
Explanation:

QUESTION NO: 582

The process of a lower court abiding by a decision of a higher court is known as:

A.
Corpus delicti

B.
Habeas corpus

C.
Ex post facto

D.
Stare decisis

E.
Mens rea

Answer: D
Explanation:

QUESTION NO: 583

The crime that consists of an unlawful entry into or remaining within a building with the intent to commit some crime therein is:

A.
Robbery

B.
Trespass

C.
Burglary

D.
Embezzlement

E.
Shoplifting

Answer: C
Explanation:

QUESTION NO: 584

Which of the following elements elevates the crime of larceny to robbery?

A.
Wrongful taking of the property of another

B.

Through the use of force or threat of force

C.
Intent to deprive the owner of the use of certain property

D.
Unlawful appropriation of property

Answer: B
Explanation:

QUESTION NO: 585

In order to make the proof of intent easier in proving shoplifting, many stores have a policy that:

A.
Requires apprehension of the suspect to be made after the accused leaves the premises

B.
Requires apprehension of the suspect as soon as the theft occurs

C.
Requires apprehension of the suspect as soon as the material is concealed

D.
Requires apprehension only upon issuance of a warrant

E.
None of the above

Answer: A
Explanation:

QUESTION NO: 586

Deadly force can only be used:

A.
In reasonable anticipation that fatal force has been threatened or is imminent against the person seeking to justify

B.
In prevention of a crime or apprehension of a criminal when a deadly weapon was employed in the commission of or attempt to commit the crime

C.
In defense of premises or property when a burglary is attempted or committed and physical force is threatened against some occupant

D.
All of the above

E.
None of the above

Answer: D
Explanation:

QUESTION NO: 587

The private citizen generally may arrest without a warrant:

A.
For a felony

B.
For a misdemeanor

C.
For a crime committed in his or her presence

D.
When he or she had "reasonable cause" to believe the person arrested committed the crime

E.
None of the above

Answer: C
Explanation:

QUESTION NO: 588

The Supreme Court decision that holds that no suspect, in a custodial environment, may be asked any questions until he or she has first been warned that he or she need not make any statement and advised of certain other rights is the:

A.
McNabb decision

B.
Mallory decision

C.
Ennis decision

D.
Miranda decision

E.
Terry decision

Answer: D
Explanation:

QUESTION NO: 589

The amendment to the U.S. Constitution that deals with searches and seizures is the:

A.
First Amendment

B.
Fourth Amendment

C.
Fifth Amendment

D.
Sixth Amendment

E.
Eighth Amendment

Answer: B
Explanation:

QUESTION NO: 590

As a general rule, searches can be made of employee lockers and desks located on the premises of the company:

A.
If consent is given by employees

B.
Under no circumstances

C.
If done by the local police

D.
If done by the security manager

E.
If done by the plant manager

Answer: A
Explanation:

QUESTION NO: 591

When a law enforcement agent induces the commission of an offense not otherwise contemplated, the accused may use an affirmative defense known as:

A.
Hearsay

B.
Illegally induced crime

C.
Ex post facto law

D.
Bill of attainder

E.
Entrapment

Answer: E
Explanation:

QUESTION NO: 592

The imputation of another's negligence to the employer is described as:

A.
Gross liability

B.
Vicarious liability

C.
Agency liability

D.
Net liability

E.
Tort liability

Answer: B
Explanation:

QUESTION NO: 593

A willful or negligent wrong done to one person by another is:

A.
A crime

B.
A misdemeanor

C.
A felony

D.
A tort

E.
A malfeasance

Answer: D
Explanation:

QUESTION NO: 594

The following action can be considered a tort:

A.
Battery

B.
False imprisonment

C.
Fraud

D.
All of the above

E.
None of the above

Answer: D
Explanation:

QUESTION NO: 595

The agency created by the Civil Rights Act of 1964 and specifically charged with investigating charges of employment discrimination that violate Title VII of the Civil Rights Act is the:

A.
Equal Employment Opportunity Commission

B.
Community Relations Commission

C.
Office of Compliance of Civil Rights

D.
Human Relations Council

E.
Civil Rights Division of the Department of Justice

Answer: A
Explanation:

QUESTION NO: 596

The area of civil law dealing with the creation and activities of independent agencies and of some executive departments of government, both federal and state, is called:

A.
Agency law

B.
Tort law

C.
Administrative law

D.
Constitutional law

E.
None of the above

Answer: C
Explanation:

QUESTION NO: 597

The codified regulations of the administrative agencies are contained in:

A.
Statutes at large

B.

The Code of Federal Regulations (CFR)

C.
The U.S. Code (USC)

D.
The Federal Register

E.
None of the above

Answer: B
Explanation:

QUESTION NO: 598

The practice of not considering evidence illegally obtained is called:

A.
The silver platter doctrine

B.
The exclusionary rule

C.
The McNabb-Mallory rule

D.
The Miranda rule

E.
The best evidence rule

Answer: B
Explanation:

QUESTION NO: 599

The privilege against self-incrimination is found in the following amendment:

A.
Fifth

B.
Tenth

C.
Second

D.
Sixth

E.
Fourteenth

Answer: A
Explanation:

QUESTION NO: 600

Corpus delicti means:

A.
The dead body

B.
The body of the crime

C.
A command to produce the body

D.
Criminal intent

E.
Criminal actions

Answer: B
Explanation:

QUESTION NO: 601

An example of a mala prohibitum crime is:

A.
Rape

B.
Illegal parking

C.
Murder

D.
Kidnapping

E.
Assault

Answer: B
Explanation:

QUESTION NO: 602

Many offenses that do not require proof of intent are called:

A.
Strict liability crimes

B.
Common-law crimes

C.
True crimes

D.
Mala in se crimes

E.
None of the above

Answer: A
Explanation:

QUESTION NO: 603

Sometimes an intent to do one act will establish the intent element for another offense, even though the act that was intended did not occur. This is:

A.
Transferred intent

B.
Felonious intent

C.
General intent

D.
Specific intent

E.
None of the above

Answer: A
Explanation:

QUESTION NO: 604

When homicide is committed by accident and misfortune in doing any lawful act by lawful means with usual ordinary caution, it is' known as:

A.
General homicide

B.
Justifiable homicide

C.
Excusable homicide

D.
Voluntary manslaughter

E.
Involuntary manslaughter

Answer: C
Explanation:

QUESTION NO: 605

A situation whereby there was adequate provocation by the victim to arouse passion and an unlawful killing took place is called:

A.
Negligent manslaughter

B.
Involuntary manslaughter

C.
Murder

D.
Voluntary manslaughter

E.
Excusable homicide

Answer: D
Explanation:

QUESTION NO: 606

Battery that mutilates or causes permanent loss of the use of a part of the body of the victim is called:

A.
Aggravated assault

B.
Aggravated battery

C.
Felonious assault

D.
Felonious battery

E.
Mayhem

Answer: E
Explanation:

QUESTION NO: 607

Whoever without lawful authority restrains an individual from going about as he or she wishes may be guilty of:

A.
False imprisonment

B.
Extortion

C.
Seduction

D.
Assault

E.
Battery

Answer: A
Explanation:

QUESTION NO: 608

The probable cause necessary to constitute a prerequisite to arrest and search by law enforcement officers is:

A.
A high degree of suspicion

B.
Evidence that will prove guilt

C.
Those facts that would lead a reasonable person to believe that the accused committed the offense

D.
A preponderance of evidence

E.
None of the above

Answer: C
Explanation:

QUESTION NO: 609

The federal agency that has primary jurisdiction over those who print and pass counterfeit money is:

A.
The FBI

B.
The Bureau of Alcohol, Tobacco, and Firearms

C.
The Secret Service

D.
The U.S. Marshal Service

E.
None of the above

Answer: C
Explanation:

QUESTION NO: 610

The federal kidnapping statute provides that:

A.

Primary jurisdiction is in the hands of the Secret Service.

B.
The FBI cannot enter the case until evidence is developed that the victim was taken across a state line.

C.
The FBI has full jurisdiction in all kidnappings, regardless of interstate transportation of the victim.

D.
A presumption is created that if the victim has not been returned within 24 hours following abduction, he or she has been moved interstate.

Answer: D
Explanation:

QUESTION NO: 611

The unlawful taking of property by force or threat of force constitutes the crime of:

A.
Burglary

B.
Robbery

C.
Assault and battery

D.
Larceny

E.
False pretenses

Answer: C
Explanation:

QUESTION NO: 612

The term used to refer to the body of the crime and all the elements necessary to prove that a crime has been committed is:

A.
Habeas corpus

B.
Corpus delicti

C.
Mens rea

D.
Actus rea

E.
None of the above

Answer: C
Explanation:

QUESTION NO: 613

One who is actually or constructively present, aiding and abetting in the commission of the crime, is generally known as a(n):

A.
Principal in the first degree

B.
Principal in the second degree

C.
Accessory before the fact

D.
Accessory after the fact

E.
None of the above

Answer: B
Explanation:

QUESTION NO: 614

One who has knowledge of the commission of a felony and render personal assistance to the felon, such as hiding him or her, i generally liable as a(n):

A.
Principal in the first degree

B.
Principal in the second degree

C.
Principal in the third degree

D.
Accessory before the fact

E.
Accessory after the fact

Answer: E
Explanation:

QUESTION NO: 615

Which of the following is not an element of a serious crime that must be proved for conviction?

A.
Motive

B.
Criminal intent

C.
Criminal act

D.
Concurrence between act and intent

E.
None of the above

Answer: A
Explanation:

QUESTION NO: 616

An offense that was not a common-law crime but created by statute is termed a(n):

A.
Mala in se crime

B.
Mala prohibitum crime

C.
Felony

D.
Misdemeanor

E.
Infraction

Answer: B
Explanation:

QUESTION NO: 617

Legislative enactments establishing arbitrary time periods in which the state must initiate criminal proceedings or not act at all are known as:

A.
Legal defenses

B.
Bills of attainder

C.
Statutes of limitation

D.
Statutes of fraud

E.
None of the above

Answer: C
Explanation:

QUESTION NO: 618

The act of inducing a person to commit a crime for the purpose of having him or her arrested is known as:

A.
Solicitation

B.
Entrapment

C.
Nolo contendere

D.
Misprision

E.
Legal suggestion

Answer: B
Explanation:

QUESTION NO: 619

As a general rule, deadly force is justified in which of the following cases?

A.
An unarmed robbery

B.
An armed robbery

C.
Observation of a man entering a second-story window of a house in the early hours of the morning

D.
In effecting the arrest of one who has committed a misdemeanor

E.
All of the above

Answer: B
Explanation:

QUESTION NO: 620

A homicide committed while attempting to effect an arrest or to prevent an escape can only be justified in:

A.
Effecting the arrest of one who has committed a misdemeanor

B.
Effecting the arrest of a fleeing felon

C.
Atrocious felony cases as an absolute last resort

D.
Affecting the arrest of any felon E

E.
All of the above

Answer: C
Explanation:

QUESTION NO: 621

Deadly force may be used to defend oneself if:

A.
One reasonably believes deadly force is necessary to protect himself or herself or another from unlawful use of deadly force of a third party

B.
One's home is broken into

C.
One is protecting one's own property

D.
All of the above

E.
None of the above

Answer: A
Explanation:

QUESTION NO: 622

Giving or attempting to give to another person an instrument known to be false with intent to defraud is:

A.
Forgery

B.
False pretenses

C.
Counterfeiting

D.
Uttering

E.
None of the above

Answer: D
Explanation:

QUESTION NO: 623

The unlawful restraint by one person of the physical liberty of another person is the crime of:

A.
Kidnapping

B.
Unlawful restraint

C.
Abduction

D.
False imprisonment

E.
None of the above

Answer: D
Explanation:

QUESTION NO: 624

In some states it is a crime to begin a criminal case without probable cause in bad faith and with the intent of harassing or injuring the other party. The crime is:

A.
Felonious intent

B.
Felonious harassment

C.
Malicious prosecution

D.
Misprision of a felony

E.
None of the above

Answer: C
Explanation:

QUESTION NO: 625

When a person in his or her private capacity and not as a public official uses written or oral threats of force or fright and demands money or property to which he or she is not entitled, the crime committed is:

A.
Blackmail

B.
Criminal defamation

C.
Bribery

D.
Misprision of a felony

E.
None of the above

Answer: A
Explanation:

QUESTION NO: 626

The corrupt procurement of another to commit perjury is:

A.
Perjury

B.
Solicitation

C.
Bribery

D.
Subornation of perjury

E.
Misprision of a felony

Answer: D
Explanation:

QUESTION NO: 627

The Federal Bureau of Investigation is under the:

A.
Treasury Department

B.
Department of the Interior

C.
Department of Defense

D.
Department of Justice

E.
State Department

Answer: D
Explanation:

QUESTION NO: 628

Federal trial courts are called:

A.
District courts

B.
Courts of Appeal

C.
Chancery courts

D.
Superior courts

E.
County courts

Answer: A
Explanation:

QUESTION NO: 629

The United States Supreme Court consists of:

A.
5 members

B.
12 members

C.
16 members

D.
7 members

E.
9 members

Answer: E
Explanation:

QUESTION NO: 630

The prohibition against being tried twice for the same crime is found in the:

A.
First Amendment of the US. Constitution

B.
Third Amendment of the US. Constitution

C.
Fifth Amendment of the US. Constitution

D.
Fourteenth Amendment of the US. Constitution

E.
None of the above

Answer: C

Explanation:

QUESTION NO: 631

In a criminal prosecution, the measure of evidence used to find the accused guilty is:

A.
Beyond a reasonable doubt

B.
Probable cause

C.
Suspicion

D.
Preponderance of evidence

Answer: A
Explanation:

QUESTION NO: 632

"Strict liability in tort" is also known as:

A.
Gross negligence

B.
Comparative negligence

C.
Intentional liability

D.
Last clear chance

E.
Liability without fault

Answer: E

Explanation:

QUESTION NO: 633

Which of the following is a mala prohibitum offense?

A.
Rape

B.
Robbery

C.
Burglary

D.
Forgery

E.
Speeding

Answer: E
Explanation:

QUESTION NO: 634

Richard Roe came home early from work and found his wife in bed with another man.

Roe become immediately incensed and killed both. He is probably guilty of:

A.
Premeditated murder

B.
Involuntary manslaughter

C.
Voluntary manslaughter

D.
Second-degree murder

E.
None of the above

Answer: C
Explanation:

QUESTION NO: 635

The U.S. Supreme Court case that established the accused's right to be informed of his or her constitutional right to remain silent, to have a lawyer present, to be informed of the right to remain silent, and of the state's duty to provide a lawyer when the accused cannot afford one is:

A.
Gideon v. Wainwright

B.
The McNabb case

C.
The Mallory case

D.
United States v. Silver Thorne

E.
Miranda v. Arizona

Answer: E
Explanation:

QUESTION NO: 636

A principal will be liable for the contracts entered into by his or her agents in emergency situations under the theory of:

A.
Agency by operation of law

B.
Agency by estoppel

C.
Constructive agency

D.
Implied agency

E.
None of the above

Answer: A
Explanation:

QUESTION NO: 637

The theory of law that vicariously imposes liability on the principal for acts of his or her agent is known as:

A.
Plain agency

B.
Master servant

C.
Strict liability

D.
Respondeat superior

E.
Common law

Answer: D
Explanation:

QUESTION NO: 638

An employer is responsible for the acts of his or her employee committed within:

A.

The employee's scope of employment

B.
The area of the place of business

C.
The employer's area of primary activity

D.
The employee's area of primary activity

E.
None of the above

Answer: A
Explanation:

QUESTION NO: 639

The doctrine that states that an employer is not liable for injuries inflicted by one employee upon another while both are engaged in the same general enterprise is called:

A.
Last clear chance

B.
Caveat emptor

C.
Respondeat superior

D.
Fellow-servant rule

E.
Workman's compensation

Answer: D
Explanation:

QUESTION NO: 640

The relationship in which two parties agree that one will act as a representative of the other is known as a(n):

A.
Contractual relationship

B.
Fiduciary relationship

C.
Partnership relationship

D.
Agency relationship

E.
None of the above

Answer: D
Explanation:

QUESTION NO: 641

An agent ordinarily can act for the principal in such a way to make the principal legally responsible provided:

A.
The agent is authorized by the principal to act that way.

B.
The agent acts reasonably.

C.
The agent notifies the principal within 24 hours,

D.
The agent is 18 years of age,

E.
All of the above.

Answer: A

Explanation:

QUESTION NO: 642

An agent can become liable while acting for the principal if:

A.
The agent violates any duties owed to the principal.

B.
The agent exceeds actual authority.

C.
The agent assumes liability for a particular transaction,

D.
All of the above.

E.
None of the above.

Answer: D
Explanation:

QUESTION NO: 643

If the agent commits a tort:

A.
The agent is personally responsible to the injured party.

B.
The agent is not liable if the agent was working for the principal at the time

C.
The agent is not liable if acting within the scope of employment.

D.
The agent is not liable if the agent has a written contract with the employer

E.
None of the above

Answer: A
Explanation:

QUESTION NO: 644

As a general rule, the employer is not liable for a tort committed by:

A.
The servant if committed in the scope of the servant's employment for the master

B.
The independent contractor

C.
One hired to do a job that is inherently dangerous

D.
None of the above

E.
All of the above

Answer: B
Explanation:

QUESTION NO: 645

If S, a subordinate, while acting within the scope of employment, injures T and T dies, S's superior:

A.
Can be held liable in a civil suit for damages

B.
Can be subjected to criminal liability

C.
Can be held liable both for a civil suit and criminal action

D.

Can be criminally liable if the act is malicious

E.
Can be criminally liable if the act is a "true" crime

Answer: A
Explanation:

QUESTION NO: 646

The requirement that certain types of contracts be in writing in order for a contract to be enforceable in a lawsuit is known as a:

A.
Contingency contract

B.
Voidable contract

C.
Statute of frauds

D.
Strict liability contract

E.
None of the above

Answer: C
Explanation:

QUESTION NO: 647

A law that sets forth a maximum time period from the happening of an event for a legal action to be properly filed in court is known as:

A.
The statute of frauds

B.
The statute of limitations

C.
The doctrine of estoppel

D.
Stare decisis

E.
None of the above

Answer: B
Explanation:

QUESTION NO: 648

A legal theory under which a person can be held liable for damage or injury even if not at fault or negligent is known as:

A.
Caveat emptor

B.
The no fault statute

C.
Strict liability

D.
Actus reus

E.
None of the above

Answer: C
Explanation:

QUESTION NO: 649

The Uniform Crime Reports are published by:

A.

The U.S. Department of Justice

B.
The Secret Service

C.
The Census Bureau

D.
The Law Enforcement Assistance Administration

E.
The FBI

Answer: E
Explanation:

QUESTION NO: 650

Crimes that do not require any mens rea (guilty intent) or negligence are commonly described as:

A.
Common-law crimes

B.
True crimes

C.
Statutory crimes

D.
Strict liability crimes

E.
None of the above

Answer: D
Explanation:

QUESTION NO: 651

It is generally held that a crime cannot be committed by a child under the age of:

A.
6

B.
7

C.
9

D.
10

E.
12

Answer: B
Explanation:

QUESTION NO: 652

The statute of limitations for the crime of murder is:

A.
Three years

B.
Five years

C.
Seven years

D.
Ten years

E.
None of the above

Answer: E
Explanation:

QUESTION NO: 653

The statute of limitations does not apply to the following:

A.
Felonies

B.
Misdemeanors

C.
While a defendant is a fugitive

D.
White-collar crimes

E.
None of the above

Answer: C
Explanation:

QUESTION NO: 654

Generally, deadly force may not be used:

A.
To solely protect property

B.
Against a mere trespasser

C.
Against a thief who steals a car

D.
All of the above

E.
None of the above

Answer: D
Explanation:

QUESTION NO: 655

In making an arrest, the authority of a private citizen is:

A.
Not as broad as a police officer's

B.
The same as a police officer's

C.
Nonexistent if the arrested person turns out to be innocent

D.
Based on the "probable cause" theory

E.
All of the above

Answer: C
Explanation:

QUESTION NO: 656

Cases in which the defendant intended to kill or inflict serious bodily injury but did not have malice because of the existence of provocation is:

A.
Voluntary manslaughter

B.
Involuntary manslaughter

C.
First-degree murder

D.
Second-degree murder

E.
Third-degree murder

Answer: A
Explanation:

QUESTION NO: 657

Cases of criminal homicide in which the actor lacked an intent to kill or cause bodily injury is:

A.
First-degree murder

B.
Second-degree murder

C.
Voluntary manslaughter

D.
Involuntary manslaughter

E.
Justifiable homicide

Answer: D
Explanation:

QUESTION NO: 658

Theft involves the crime of:

A.
Robbery

B.
Embezzlement

C.
Larceny

D.
False pretenses

E.
All of the above

Answer: E
Explanation:

QUESTION NO: 659

The legal standard that must be met to sustain an arrest is known as:

A.
Proof beyond a reasonable doubt

B.
Probable cause

C.
Suspicion

D.
Preponderance of evidence

E.
None of the above

Answer: B
Explanation:

QUESTION NO: 660

The amendment that provides that no person shall be denied life, liberty, or property without due process of law is the:

A.
First Amendment

B.
Second Amendment

C.

Fifth Amendment

D.
Eighth Amendment

E.
Fourteenth Amendment

Answer: C
Explanation:

QUESTION NO: 661

The right to have the assistance of counsel for one's defense is provided by the:

A.
Second Amendment

B.
Fifth Amendment

C.
Sixth Amendment

D.
Eighth Amendment

E.
Tenth Amendment

Answer: C
Explanation:

QUESTION NO: 662

Police are allowed to conduct a frisk-type search where there was reason to believe the person stopped was armed according to the Supreme Court decision of:

A.
Terry v. Ohio

B.
Mapp v. Ohio

C.
Kirby v. Illinois

D.
Massiah v. U.S.

E.
Wong Sun v. U.S.

Answer: A
Explanation:

QUESTION NO: 663

A legal search may be made:

A.
Without a warrant

B.
Incident to lawful arrest

C.
With consent

D.
For inventory purposes

E.
All of the above

Answer: E
Explanation:

QUESTION NO: 664

For a search warrant to be valid, it must conform to the following requirement(s):

A.
It may be issued only for certain objects.

B.
It must be issued on probable cause.

C.
The place to be searched and things to be seized must be particularly described.

D.
All of the above.

E.
None of the above.

Answer: D
Explanation:

QUESTION NO: 665

Which of the following is an exception to the general rule that a search and seizure requires a warrant?

A.
Waiver

B.
Movable vehicle

C.
Seizure without a search (plain view)

D.
All of the above

E.
None of the above

Answer: D
Explanation:

QUESTION NO: 666

Two famous Supreme Court rulings resulted in a rule of law that states that a person upon arrest shall be taken before a judicial officer for arraignment without unnecessary delay. The rule is called the:

A.
McNabb-Mallory rule

B.
Miranda rule

C.
Terry v. Ohio rule

D.
Escobedo rule

E.
Katz rule

Answer: A
Explanation:

QUESTION NO: 667

Which of the following procedures has been held to violate the self-incrimination provisions of the Fifth Amendment?

A.
Fingerprinting for identification purposes

B.
Photographing for identification purposes

C.
Pre-indictment lineup

D.
All of the above

E.
None of the above

Answer: E

Explanation:

QUESTION NO: 668

Which of the following is not considered to be personal property?

A.
Cars

B.
Animals

C.
Money

D.
Furniture

E.
House

Answer: E
Explanation:

QUESTION NO: 669

Which of the following crimes would be considered a white-collar crime?

A.
Tax evasion

B.
False advertising

C.
Mail fraud

D.
All of the above

E.
None of the above

Answer: D
Explanation:

QUESTION NO: 670

What is the crime when a person, knowing an object to be false, attempts to pass it off as the real thing?

A.
Forgery

B.
False pretenses

C.
Uttering

D.
Larceny by trick

E.
None of the above

Answer: C
Explanation:

QUESTION NO: 671

The investigative jurisdiction for the federal crime of counterfeiting is in the hands of the:

A.
FBI

B.
Secret Service

C.
Internal Revenue Service

D.
Bureau of Alcohol, Tobacco, and Firearms

E.
None of the above

Answer: B
Explanation:

QUESTION NO: 672

To combat the crime of loan sharking, the U.S. Congress passed:

A.
The Organized Crime Control Act

B.
The Extortionate Credit Transactions Act

C.
The Omnibus Crime Act

D.
The Federal Crime Act

E.
None of the above

Answer: B
Explanation:

QUESTION NO: 673

Which of the following is not considered to be an inchoate crime?

A.
Attempt

B.
Solicitation

C.
Conspiracy

D.
Embezzlement

E.
All of the above

Answer: D
Explanation:

QUESTION NO: 674

The procedure by which a defendant in a criminal case petitions the court to allow an inspection of certain items in the possession of the prosecution is known as:

A.
Venue

B.
Estoppel

C.
Voir dire

D.
Discovery

E.
None of the above

Answer: D
Explanation:

QUESTION NO: 675

The term "venue" refers to:

A.
The authority of the court to deal with a particular case

B.

The place at which the authority of the court should be exercised

C.
The process of jury selection

D.
The process of appeal

E.
None of the above

Answer: B
Explanation:

QUESTION NO: 676

The examination of prospective jurors on the jury panel is commonly referred to as:

A.
Discovery

B.
Voir dire

C.
Venue

D.
Peremptory challenge

E.
Mittimus

Answer: B
Explanation:

QUESTION NO: 677

A challenge of a prospective juror for no specific reason is known as:

A.

Discovery

B.
Examination in chief

C.
Peremptory challenge

D.
Challenge without cause

E.
Voir dire

Answer: C
Explanation:

QUESTION NO: 678

Which of the following is not recommended as a witness in a court of law?

A.
Sit erect, with ankles crossed and hands folded on your lap.

B.
Look up to judge from time to time.

C.
Seek opportunity to smile genuinely.

D.
Fold your arms across your chest.

E.
Watch attorney as he or she frames a question.

Answer: D
Explanation:

QUESTION NO: 679

The attitude of the U.S. Department of Justice with regard to introducing polygraph results as evidence is that the:

A.
Justice Department opposes it

B.
Justice Department will allow it

C.
Justice Department feels it is okay if a waiver is given

D.
Justice Department feels failure to take a polygraph is evidence of guilt

E.
Judge should be present during the polygraph examination

Answer: A
Explanation:

QUESTION NO: 680

Occupational Safety and Health Administration (OSHA) regulations have been in force since:

A.
1940

B.
1951

C.
1970

D.
1971

E.
1980

Answer: D
Explanation:

QUESTION NO: 681

OSHA is administered by the:

A.
Department of Health and Human Resources

B.
Department of Labor

C.
Department of the Interior

D.
Department of Justice

E.
Department of Commerce

Answer: B
Explanation:

QUESTION NO: 682

As a practical matter, the OSHA Act covers

A.
Only federal workers

B.
Nongovernmental employers that manufacture hazardous materials

C.
Nongovernmental employers whose activities affect commerce

D.
Those employers in the mining industry only

E.
None of the above

Answer: C

Explanation:

QUESTION NO: 683

Which of the following was not provided by the OSHA Act?

A.
An effective enforcement program

B.
Reporting procedures

C.
Research

D.
Authorization for the Secretary of the Interior to set mandatory standards

E.
Development of safety standards

Answer: D
Explanation:

QUESTION NO: 684

Under the OSHA Act, a national consensus standard was defined as one that is:

A.
Adopted and issued by a nationally recognized standard-producing organization such as NFPA

B.
Developed after consideration of conflicting or differing views

C.
In the nature of a practice designated by the Secretary of Labor after consultation with other federal agencies

D.
All of the above

E.
None of the above

Answer: D
Explanation:

QUESTION NO: 685

The OSHA Act allows states to continue their present safety and health enforcement activities provided that:

A.
The state program is "at least as effective" as the federal program

B.
The Secretary of Labor signs a certificate of authorization

C.
The attorney general after hearing approves

D.
Litigation is pursued in the federal court system

E.
None of the above

Answer: A
Explanation:

QUESTION NO: 686

A "de minimis" violation of the OSHA Act is:

A.
One that is serious

B.
One that is serious and willful

C.

One that is willful

D.
One that has no immediate or direct relationship to safety or health

E.
One that is repeated

Answer: D
Explanation:

QUESTION NO: 687

Citations issued by an OSHA area director are:

A.
Written

B.
Mailed by U.S. certified mail

C.
Required to be posted at or near the place of violation

D.
All of the above

E.
None of the above

Answer: D
Explanation:

QUESTION NO: 688

Which of the following is not required by OSHA regulations?

A.
A serious violation must be assessed a monetary penalty.

B.
A nonserious violation may be assessed a proposed penalty.

C.
All notices, including de minimis notices, must be posted.

D.
Written notices must be sent to the employer whenever penalties are proposed.

Answer: C
Explanation:

QUESTION NO: 689

Under OSHA regulations, a serious violation must be assessed some monetary penalty but the amount should not exceed:

A.
$100,000

B.
$1,000,000

C.
$50,000

D.
$10,000

E.
$1000

Answer: E
Explanation:

QUESTION NO: 690

Unless appealed, payment of penalties under OSHA must be made within:

A.

10 working days

B.
5 working days

C.
15 working days

D.
30 working days

E.
2 months

Answer: C
Explanation:

QUESTION NO: 691

In order to enforce compliance with safety and health standards under OSHA, employees are:

A.
Required to comply within 5 days of written notice

B.
Required to pay $10,000 per day for each day of noncompliance

C.
Required to comply or to forfeit job

D.
All of the above

E.
None of the above

Answer: E
Explanation:

QUESTION NO: 692

The OSHA law requires the maintenance of three basic types of injury and illness records by each establishment that employs:

A.
5 or more employees

B.
8 or more employees

C.
15 or more employees

D.
50 or more employees

E.
200 or more employees

Answer: B
Explanation:

QUESTION NO: 693

Under OSHA regulations, the employer is responsible to see that every recordable injury or illness is listed on the log within:

A.
4 days of learning of occurrence

B.
6 days of learning of occurrence

C.
14 days of learning of occurrence

D.
15 days of learning of occurrence

E.
30 days of learning of occurrence

Answer: B
Explanation:

QUESTION NO: 694

The law that prohibits the armed forces from executing civil law in the United States, its territories, and possessions is:

A.
Title 18, U.S. Code

B.
The Delimitations Agreement

C.
The Armed Services Act of 1950

D.
The Posse Comitatus Act

E.
None of the above

Answer: D
Explanation:

QUESTION NO: 695

The federal criminal law is set forth in the following title of the U.S. Code:

A.
Title 5

B.
Title 12

C.
Title 18

D.
Title 28

E.
Title 50

Answer: C
Explanation:

QUESTION NO: 696

According to the U.S. Code, a felony is:

A.
Any offense punishable by death

B.
Any offense punishable by imprisonment of one year or more

C.
Any offense punishable by imprisonment exceeding one year

D.
Any offense punishable by death or imprisonment for a term exceeding one year

E.
None of the above

Answer: D
Explanation:

QUESTION NO: 697

The act of concealing the commission of a felony cognizable by a U.S. court by someone having knowledge of the felony is a violation called:

A.
Misprision of felony

B.
Accessory

C.
Subornation of perjury

D.
Obstruction of justice

E.
None of the above

Answer: A
Explanation:

QUESTION NO: 698

The Fourth Amendment of the U.S. Constitution does not apply to:

A.
Secret Service agent searches

B.
U.S. Customs agents searches

C.
A search by a private person

D.
A search by an FBI agent

E.
A search by local police

Answer: C
Explanation:

QUESTION NO: 699

When a law enforcement agent induces the commission of an offense, the process is called:

A.
Accessory before the fact

B.
Misprision of a felony

C.
Entrapment

D.
Stare decisis

E.
Corpus delecti

Answer: C
Explanation:

QUESTION NO: 700

Statements by persons that things done or said by them are actually as they are described or said to be constitute:

A.
Expressed contracts

B.
Warranties

C.
Implied contracts

D.
All of the above

E.
None of the above

Answer: B
Explanation:

QUESTION NO: 701

The actual use of force against another, which involves physical touching, is a willful tort called in common law:

A.
Assault

B.
Battery

C.
Felonious assault

D.
Aggravated assault

E.
None of the above

Answer: B
Explanation:

QUESTION NO: 702

Wrongful appropriation of the personal property of another to the use of the taker is a tort called:

A.
Conversion

B.
Larceny

C.
Trespass

D.
Embezzlement

E.
None of the above

Answer: A
Explanation:

QUESTION NO: 703

Rules issued by administrative agencies are published in the:

A.
Congressional Record

B.
Federal Register

C.
U.S. Code

D.
Statutes at large

E.
None of the above

Answer: B
Explanation:

QUESTION NO: 704

Rules promulgated by administrative agencies are ultimately published in the:

A.
Code of Federal Regulations

B.
U.S. Code

C.
Federal Register

D.
Statutes at large

E.
Congressional Record

Answer: A
Explanation:

QUESTION NO: 705

A writ issued by a court directing the recipient to appear and testify is a:

A.
Warrant

B.
Subpoena

C.
Writ of mandamus

D.
Writ of prohibition

E.
None of the above

Answer: B
Explanation:

QUESTION NO: 706

The process whereby the determinations and actions of an administrative agency are reviewed by the courts is:

A.
Stare decisis

B.
Certiorari

C.
Mandamus

D.
Judicial review

E.
None of the above

Answer: D

Explanation:

QUESTION NO: 707

The Act that deals with the release and disclosure of certain kinds of information by the federal government is:

A.
The Freedom of Information Act

B.
The Privacy Act

C.
The Administrative Procedures Act

D.
The Federal Communications Act

E.
None of the above

Answer: A
Explanation:

QUESTION NO: 708

The Freedom of Information Act, passed in 1966, applies to:

A.
State governments

B.
State and federal governments

C.
Private industry

D.
The federal government only

E.
None of the above

Answer: D
Explanation:

QUESTION NO: 709

Which of the following is not subject to public disclosure under the Freedom of Information Act?

A.
Classified information

B.
Internal personnel rules

C.
Personal medical records

D.
Confidential informants

E.
All of the above

Answer: E
Explanation:

QUESTION NO: 710

When guards are deputized, it is customary and prudent to:

A.
Encourage the guard to assist law enforcement off the premises

B.
Take out additional liability insurance

C.
Limit the scope of the guard's authority to the actual guard duties

D.
All of the above

E.
None of the above

Answer: C
Explanation:

QUESTION NO: 711

An arrest made by a guard who has not been deputized is called:

A.
A citizen's arrest

B.
A conservator's arrest

C.
An illegal arrest

D.
A detention

E.
None of the above

Answer: A
Explanation:

QUESTION NO: 712

The general rule as to the amount of force a guard is permitted to use in order to accomplish a lawful arrest is:

A.
The amount needed to ensure the guard is not injured

B.

Up to and including deadly force

C.
The maximum amount

D.
Only such force as is reasonably necessary

Answer: D
Explanation:

QUESTION NO: 713

The authority of a private person to make an arrest is usually:

A.
Unlimited

B.
Limited to those cases where a warrant is obtained

C.
A matter of state law

D.
The same as a deputized guard

E.
None of the above

Answer: C
Explanation:

QUESTION NO: 714

Which of the following is not true of common law?

A.
It originated in France.

B.
It was brought to America by English colonists.

C.
It basically was unwritten law.

D.
All of the above.

E.
None of the above.

Answer: A
Explanation:

QUESTION NO: 715

The makeup of a federal grand jury is:

A.
16-23 jurors

B.
12 jurors

C.
12-18 jurors

D.
5 jurors

E.
9 jurors

Answer: A
Explanation:

QUESTION NO: 716

Which of the following is not correct with regard to the grand jury?

A.
A federal grand jury consists of 16-23 jurors.

B.
A witness may be accompanied by his or her attorney.

C.
The proceedings are secret.

D.
Its main responsibility is to find probable cause.

E.
None of the above.

Answer: B
Explanation:

QUESTION NO: 717

If a grand jury determines that probable cause exists and that the accused committed a crime, the grand jury then:

A.
Issues an information

B.
Issues an indictment

C.
Issues a mittimus

D.
Enters a finding of guilty

E.
None of the above

Answer: B
Explanation:

QUESTION NO: 718

A case that is proved "on the face of it" is known as:

A.
A corpus delicti case

B.
A prima facie case

C.
The case in chief

D.
A directed verdict

E.
None of the above

Answer: B
Explanation:

QUESTION NO: 719

Which of the following would be considered a primary tort relevant to security officers?

A.
Battery

B.
Assault

C.
False imprisonment

D.
All of the above

E.
None of the above

Answer: C
Explanation:

QUESTION NO: 720

Limitations may be imposed on authority of a security force by:

A.
Licensing laws

B.
Administrative regulations

C.
Specific statutes

D.
All of the above

E.
None of the above

Answer: D
Explanation:

QUESTION NO: 721

A legal doctrine that holds that the master is responsible for the actions of his servant while his servant is acting in his master's behalf is known as:

A.
Caveat emptor

B.
Vicarious liability

C.
Strict liability

D.
Respondeat superior

E.
None of the above

Answer: D
Explanation:

QUESTION NO: 722

Which of the following torts affects private security and investigative personnel?

A.
False imprisonment

B.
Malicious prosecution

C.
Invasion of privacy

D.
Trespass on personal property

E.
All of the above

Answer: E
Explanation:

QUESTION NO: 723

Which of the following is generally not true with regard to the constitutional limitation on arrest powers of private police?

A.
A private police agent operates under the same constitutional limitations as public police.

B.
A private policeman's authority is essentially the same as a private citizen's.

C.
Regulation of authority of private police will usually be based on state law.

D.

All of the above.

E.
None of the above.

Answer: A
Explanation:

QUESTION NO: 724

A police officer may make an arrest without a warrant:

A.
When he or she witnesses a misdemeanor or felony

B.
When a felony is committed and the officer has reasonable cause to believe a suspect committed it

C.
When he or she has reasonable cause to believe a felony was committed and reasonable cause to believe the suspect committed it

D.
When he or she has reasonable cause to believe the suspect is an escaped convict

E.
All of the above

Answer: A
Explanation:

QUESTION NO: 725

Which of the following is not true with regard to arrest by a private citizen?

A.
Private Citizens may arrest for a misdemeanor only if they witnessed it.

B.

Private Citizens may arrest if a felony has been committed and they have reasonable cause to believe a suspect has committed it.

C.
Private Citizens may make an arrest if they have reasonable cause to believe a felony has been committed.

D.
All of the above

E.
None of the above

Answer: C
Explanation:

QUESTION NO: 726

The most common charge placed against someone who has made an erroneous arrest is:

A.
Kidnapping

B.
False imprisonment

C.
Assault and battery

D.
Malicious prosecution

E.
None of the above

Answer: B
Explanation:

QUESTION NO: 727

Which of the following is true with regard to the power of detention?

A.
Detention differs from arrest.

B.
It is lawful as long as it is for a reasonable time and conducted reasonably.

C.
There is no one standard to apply.

D.
All of the above.

E.
None of the above.

Answer: D
Explanation:

QUESTION NO: 728

Which of the following is true with regard to the law of arrest?

A.
Force may be used if it is reasonable and necessary.

B.
The deputized private agent has powers similar to the police.

C.
Citizen's arrest is not a right, it is a privilege.

D.
The private security agent should understand what his or her powers and limitations are according to law.

E.
All of the above.

Answer: E
Explanation:

QUESTION NO: 729

A private citizen may arrest in which of the following cases?

A.
When a felony has been committed and he or she has reason to believe that a suspect has committed it

B.
When he or she has reasonable cause to believe that a felony has been committed and reasonable cause to believe that the suspect committed it

C.
When he or she has reason to believe that a suspect is an escaped convict or has violated parole or probation

D.
All of the above

E.
None of the above

Answer: A
Explanation:

QUESTION NO: 730

Defenses and immunities that protect a person from liability resulting from a private arrest include:

A.
Self-defense

B.
Defense of property

C.
Crime prevention

D.
All of the above

E.

None of the above

Answer: D
Explanation:

QUESTION NO: 731

Generally, a private citizen has the right to initiate arrest for a misdemeanor if the:

A.
Misdemeanor was in fact committed

B.
Misdemeanor was committed in the arrester's presence

C.
Private citizen's rights to arrest do not apply to misdemeanors

D.
All of the above

E.
None of the above

Answer: B
Explanation:

QUESTION NO: 732

When armed with a pistol, the private security officer should use it to immobilize a suspect:

A.
At first sign of resistance

B.
Only as a last resort

C.
Under no circumstances

D.
All of the above

E.
None of the above

Answer: B
Explanation:

QUESTION NO: 733

If a private security officer violates the restriction of the laws of arrest that apply to him or her, he or she may:

A.
Jeopardize the case against the subject

B.
Be subject to criminal charges

C.
Be held liable for damages in a civil suit

D.
All of the above

E.
None of the above

Answer: D
Explanation:

QUESTION NO: 734

A preliminary examination in a court proceeding to determine if a prospective juror is qualified to sit on a jury panel is called:

A.
Arraignment

B.
Preliminary hearing

C.
Voir dire

D.
Discovery

E.
None of the above

Answer: C
Explanation:

QUESTION NO: 735

A sworn statement of a party or witness taken outside the court after notice is given to the opposing side, which provides information or evidence to a court is:

A.
An affidavit

B.
A deposition

C.
A writ of mandamus

D.
A writ of certiorari

E.
None of the above

Answer: B
Explanation:

QUESTION NO: 736

For a search with voluntary consent to be valid, the person being searched must:

A.
Be aware of his or her rights

B.
Not be coerced in any way

C.
Be the person giving the consent

D.
Give consent in writing whenever possible

E.
All of the above

Answer: E
Explanation:

QUESTION NO: 737

A valid arrest must contain the following elements:

A.
Intent of taking person into physical custody

B.
Authority on the part of arresting officer

C.
Physical control by arresting officer

D.
Understanding by person who is being arrested

E.
All of the above

Answer: E
Explanation:

QUESTION NO: 738

According to the Hallcrest I study, published in 1985, employees in various facets of private security in the United States number about:

A.
500,000

B.
700,000

C.
1,000,000

D.
3,000,000

Answer: C
Explanation:

QUESTION NO: 739

According to Hallcrest I, the common ground for interaction between law enforcement and private resources is:

A.
Education

B.
Patriotism

C.
Career enhancement

D.
Crime

Answer: D
Explanation:

QUESTION NO: 740

According to estimates made by the Fireman's Fund Insurance Company, about one third of all business failures are caused by:

A.
Thefts by outsiders (nonemployees)

B.
Thefts by employees

C.
Mismanagement

D.
Poor quality of product

Answer: B
Explanation:

QUESTION NO: 741

Private security relies on both commercial security services and government agencies for intelligence gathering and crisis management planning. Which of the following agencies has overall coordinating responsibility for the federal government in the event of a large-scale disruption of social, economic, or political significance due to a massive terrorist or nuclear incident?

A.
The CIA

B.
The FBI

C.
FEMA

D.
The Secret Service

Answer: C
Explanation:

QUESTION NO: 742

Hallcrest I stated that the major item conspicuously absent from police-based crime prevention programs was:

A.
A comprehensive training program

B.
Manpower dedicated to crime prevention concepts

C.
The input of a huge number of persons employed in private security

D.
The use of updated technology

Answer: C
Explanation:

QUESTION NO: 743

According to Hallcrest I, what was the most frequent recommendation made by both law enforcement and security managers to improve private security officials and their working relationships with the police?

A.
Higher entry-level pay

B.
Upgrading quality of security personnel

C.
A planned educational program involving both police and private security

D.
Requirement of being armed

Answer: B
Explanation:

QUESTION NO: 744

Hallcrest I indicates that the most frequently shared resource between law enforcement and private security is:

A.
A CCTV system and other surveillance equipment

B.
Personnel

C.
"Buy money" for stolen goods

D.
Reward money

Answer: B
Explanation:

QUESTION NO: 745

The main objective of private security is:

A.
To apprehend those who steal property from their firms

B.
To protect assets and prevent losses

C.
To assist police in investigation of crimes

D.
To prevent unauthorized persons from entry on firm's property

Answer: B
Explanation:

QUESTION NO: 746

What is the most frequently investigated crime by private security?

A.
Employee theft

B.
Shoplifting

C.
Bad checks

D.
Embezzlement

Answer: A
Explanation:

QUESTION NO: 747

As a general rule, local law enforcement has very little effect on many crimes against business. However, there are some crimes that would be the exception.

Which of the following would be the exception to this general rule?

A.
Shoplifting

B.
Employee theft

C.
Embezzlement

D.
Burglary

Answer: D
Explanation:

QUESTION NO: 748

Approximately what percentage of medium and large security departments deputize private security personnel or give them special police powers?

A.
10 percent

B.
25 percent

C.
50 percent

D.
60 percent

Answer: B
Explanation:

QUESTION NO: 749

A Hallcrest I survey was made relative to private security perceptions of law enforcement cooperation of criminal incidents and assistance calls. The survey showed that proprietary security managers perceived the degree of law enforcement cooperation to be:

A.
Don't cooperate

B.
Cooperate reluctantly

C.
Cooperate fully

D.
Interfere with the private security investigation

Answer: C
Explanation:

QUESTION NO: 750

According to Hallcrest I, approximately what percentage of proprietary security employees feel the public police are satisfied with their current level of involvement in problems referred by security personnel?

A.
10 percent

B.
20 percent

C.
40 percent

D.
60 percent

Answer: D
Explanation:

QUESTION NO: 751

Hallcrest I revealed that operational law enforcement employees rated their overall relationships with private security as:

A.
Very good or excellent

B.
Bad

C.
Poor

D.
Just moderately good

Answer: A
Explanation:

QUESTION NO: 752

Hallcrest I revealed that chiefs and sheriffs rated their overall relationships with private security as:

A.
Excellent

B.
Very good

C.
Extremely bad

D.
Poor or less than good

Answer: D
Explanation:

QUESTION NO: 753

According to Hallcrest II, American businesses' losses to crime in 1990 were estimated at:

A.
$114 billion

B.
$53 billion

C.
$241 billion

D.
$16 billion

Answer: A
Explanation:

QUESTION NO: 754

A national crime survey for the years 1975-1988 reported that the percentage of households touched by crime had:

A.
Increased by 25 percent

B.
Decreased by 23 percent

C.
Increased by 7 percent

D.
Decreased by 5 percent

Answer: B
Explanation:

QUESTION NO: 755

For the past 20 years, the two major components of economic crime have been:

A.
Employee theft and corporate bribery

B.
Fraud and embezzlement

C.
White-collar crime and ordinary crime

D.
Computer crime and ordinary crime

Answer: C
Explanation:

QUESTION NO: 756

According to the White House Conference for a Drug-Free America, approximately how many Americans had used an illegal drug in 1987?

A.
1 in 20

B.
1 in 2

C.
1 in 7

D.
1 in 40

Answer: C
Explanation:

QUESTION NO: 757

According to a 1989 Gallup Poll, what percentage of American' workers have personal knowledge of co-workers using illegal drugs on the job?

A.
5 percent

B.
10 percent

C.
25 percent

D.
50 percent

Answer: C
Explanation:

QUESTION NO: 758

The percentage of the world's production of illegal drugs consumed in the United States is approximately:

A.
5 percent

B.
25 percent

C.
60 percent

D.
95 percent

Answer: C
Explanation:

QUESTION NO: 759

The total annual cost to the United States for drug abuse due to resulting crime, lost productivity, absenteeism, health care costs, and so forth is most closely represented by:

A.
$50 million

B.
$100 million

C.
$100 billion

D.
$400 billion

Answer: C
Explanation:

QUESTION NO: 760

According to a 1989 Department of Labor study, the percentage of employees in America working for a company that has a drug-testing program for employees or plans to have a drug-testing program is:

A.
1 percent

B.
10 percent

C.
50 percent

D.
80 percent

Answer: B
Explanation:

QUESTION NO: 761

To improve cooperation and communications between private security and law enforcement, the authors of Hallcrest II recommend that:

A.
Cooperative programs be established in every metropolitan area

B.
Cities and counties enact ordinances providing for the police to regulate security

C.
Secondary employment of law enforcement officers in security work be prohibited

D.
Police academies teach security officers more about police work

Answer: A
Explanation:

QUESTION NO: 762

The percentage of computer security incidents resulting from "insider" attacks by dishonest and disgruntled employees is approximately:

A.

10 percent

B.
35 percent

C.
50 percent

D.
80 percent

Answer: D
Explanation:

QUESTION NO: 763

The percentage of computer security incidents that are annually believed to be attributed to hackers is closest to:

A.
1 percent

B.
10 percent

C.
20 percent

D.
50 percent

Answer: A
Explanation:

QUESTION NO: 764

A 1990 National Institute of Justice study indicated that what percentage of computer crimes are not prosecuted?

A.

10 percent

B.
25 percent

C.
70 percent

D.
90 percent

Answer: D
Explanation:

QUESTION NO: 765

The practice of preventing unauthorized persons from gammg intelligent information by analyzing electromagnetic emanations from electronic equipment, such as computers, is often termed:

A.
Tempest

B.
Veiling

C.
Bugging

D.
Hardening

Answer: A
Explanation:

QUESTION NO: 766

According to Hallcrest II, North American incidents of terrorism represent what percentage of worldwide incidents?

A.
Less than 1 percent

B.
About 10 percent

C.
Almost 25 percent

D.
40 percent

Answer: A
Explanation:

QUESTION NO: 767

Since 1985, the number of international terrorist incidents occurring each year is closest to:

A.
1000

B.
5000

C.
10,000

D.
20,000

Answer: A
Explanation:

Printed in Poland
by Amazon Fulfillment
Poland Sp. z o.o., Wrocław

29060427R00237